Welsh Place Names

DEWI DAVIES

Welsh Place Names

and their meanings

This edition: 2016

Cover design: Y Lolfa

ISBN: 9 781 84771 313 1

FSC

Published and printed in Wales
on paper from well managed forests by
Y Lolfa Cyf., Talybont, Ceredigion SY24 5HE
e-mail ylolfa@ylolfa.com
website www.ylolfa.com
tel 01970 832 304
fax 832 782

Foreword

Many people are interested in Welsh placenames and their meanings. Wherever we go in Wales we are surrounded by them and they often serve as a link between the past and the present. No country is able to boast of more beautiful placenames than Wales and to the visitor to our country they are a sign that he or she is in a land which has a language and culture different from any other.

In this book I have gathered together some 2,500 placenames including parishes, towns, villages and farms as well as many other geographical features. Lack of space prevents me from including more.

Many of the names are very old and it is difficult in some cases, even impossible at times, to arrive at their true meanings. Long usage has played havoc with them both in spelling and pronunciation. Nevertheless, the placenames in this book are, for the most part, ones about which we can be reasonably sure as to their meanings.

A note on the pronunciation of Welsh letters has also been included as well as an explanation as to why words in the placenames sometimes change.

Pronunciation of Welsh Alphabet

b, d, h, l, m, n, p, t, are sounded as in English
c as in "**k**ing"; ch as in "lo**ch**";
dd, as in "**th**at"; f, as in "**v**ase";
ff, as in "**f**arm"; g, as in "**g**ame";
r, well trilled; s, as in "**s**ong";
ng, as in "so**ng**"; ph, as in "**ph**oto";
rh, trilled with h. th, as in "**th**rough".
ll is more easily learnt by oral example.

Welsh vowels, a, e, i, o, u, w, y, can be both long and short.

a, as in f**a**rm and c**a**n;
e, as in l**a**te and w**e**t;
i, as in h**ee**l and p**i**t;
o, as in fl**oo**r and c**o**t;
u, usually like long "**i**";
w, as in sch**oo**l and g**oo**d;
y, as in g**u**n and p**i**t.

Welsh words of two syllables and over usually have the emphasis on the last
syllable but one.

Word Changes

It will be seen that many of the Welsh words change from their original form. These changes occur both in spelling and pronunciation. This is mainly because:—

1. Rules of mutation—

Most feminine nouns mutate when preceded by the definite article, y, yr, 'r (the)

e.g. melin (mill) — y felin (the mill);
gwaun (meadow) — y waun (the meadow);
derwen (oak) — y dderwen (the oaks);
coeden (tree) — y goeden (the tree).

Sometimes, though incorrectly, the definite article is omitted though the feminine noun is still mutated.

e.g. Felindre for Y Felindre
Groesffordd for Y Groesffordd.

Adjectives mutate when describing a feminine noun.

e.g. Heol-las for Heol (glas);
Neuadd-lwyd for Neuadd-(llwyd);
Nant-ddu for Nant-(du).

2. Change because of usage or dialect :

e.g.: dole for dolau;
ffalde for ffaldau;
hewl for heol;
tre for tref;
isha for isaf;
dou for dau.

3. Because of contraction :

e.g.: tyn for tyddyn;

4. English influence:

e.g.: avon for afon; gare for gaer;
oyre for oer or aur; wrlod for gweirglodd.

Parishes, Towns, etc.

Abbey Cwm-hir :	abbey of the long valley;
Aber :	1. a small stream;
	2. confluence of a river or stream;
Aberaeron :	mouth of river Aeron (name of goddess);
Aberangell :	mouth of river Angell (tributary);
Aber-arth :	mouth of river Arth (bear or headland);
Aberbechan :	mouth or river Bechan (small);
Aber-brân :	mouth of river Brân (dark water);
Abercamddwr :	mouth of river Camddwr (winding);
Abercegyr :	mouth of river Cegyr (hemlock);
Aber-craf :	mouth of river Craf (garlic);
Aberdaron :	mouth of river Daron (dar - oak trees);
Aberdauddwr :	mouth of the two waters;
Aberdovey (Aberdyfi) :	mouth of river Dyfi (dark);
Aberedw :	mouth of river Edw;
Abererch :	mouth of greyish-blue river;
Aberffraw (-ffro) :	mouth of abundant, flowing river,
Aber-ffrwd :	mouth of stream;
Abergavenny (y Fenni) :	mouth of river Gavenny (from gof-smith);
Abergele :	gelau—stream similar to blade of sword;
Aberglanhiron :	mouth of river Glanhiron;
Aberglaslyn :	mouth of river Glaslyn (green valley);
Abergorlech :	mouth of river Gorlech (rocky);
Abergwili :	river Gwili (pers. name — happy, gentle);
Abergwydol :	mouth of river Gwydol;
Abergwynant :	mouth of river Gwynant (fair stream or valley);
Abergynolwyn :	mouth of river Gynolwyn (pers. name);
Aberhafesp :	mouth of river Hafesp (one that dries up);
Aberhenllan :	mouth of river Henllan (old church);
Aberhiriaeth :	mouth of river Hiriaeth (long ridge);
Aberhosan :	mouth of river Rhosan (moorland river);
Aberhydfer :	mouth of river Hydfer (bold stream);
Aberithon :	mouth of river Ithon (name of goddess);
Aberllefenni :	mouth of river Llefenni (elm trees);
Aberllynfi :	mouth of river Llynfi (smoothly-flowing);
Abermagwr :	mouth of river Magwr (among rocks);
Abermarchnant :	mouth of river Marchnant (horse stream);
Aber-mule :	mouth of river Miwl;
Aber-naint :	mouth of the streams;
Aber-nant :	mouth of stream;
Aber-porth :	mouth of river; porth harbour;
Abersoch :	mouth of river Soch;
Aberysgir :	mouth of river Ysgir (ridge);
Aberystwyth :	mouth of river Ystwyth (winding);

Adfa :	border; recess; place to drive animals;
Adwy-wynt :	wind gap:
afon :	a river;
Aithnen :	poplar tree;
allt (or gallt) :	hillside or wood;
Allt Cae Melyn :	hillside of yellow field;
Allt Cae Du :	hillside of black field;
Allt Dolanog :	hillside of winding river;
Allt Dderw :	oak wood;
Allt Ddu :	black hillside;
Allt Fran Ddu :	hillside of black crow;
Allt-goch :	red hillside;
Allt-lwyd :	brown or grey hillside or wood;
Allt-mawr :	big hillside or wood;
Alltuchaf :	highest hillside or wood;
Alltwalis :	hillside of Walis (pers.name);
Allt-wen :	white or fair ascent;
Alltwnog :	hillside or wood of Wnog (pers. name);
Alltyddinas :	hillside of the fort;
Alltyffynnon :	hillside of the spring;
Allt y Gadair :	hillside of the fort (or chair);
Allt y Genlli :	hillside of the hawk;
Allt y Gribin :	hillside of the ridge;
Allt y Maen :	hillside of the rock;
Allt y Moch :	hillside of the pigs (or swift brook);
Allt yr Eryr :	hillside of the eagle;
Allt yr Hendre :	hillside of the old home;
Amlwch :	near water;
Amroth (Amrath) :	near the mound or fort;
Aran :	mountain ridge;
Ardwyn :	on a hill;
Arddleen (Gardd-lin) :	flax garden;
Arddu, yr :	the dark high land;
Arennig :	hillside or ridge;
Argoed :	by a wood;
Arthog :	prob. land of the bears or headlands;
Arwystli :	land of Arwystl (pers. name);
bach :	1. small;
	2. river bend or nook;
Bachelldre :	home of small nook;
Bach Howey (Hywi) :	bend of river Hywi;
Bachie :	river bends; nooks;
Bagillt :	field of Bacga (pers. name);
Bailey Bedw (Beili) :	birch enclosure;
Bailey Heulwen (Beili) :	enclosure of sunshine;
Beili-mawr :	big enclosure;
Beili Neuadd :	enclosure of the hall;

Bala :	place where river flows from a lake;
banadl :	broom;
banc :	mound, bank or hillock;
Banc Du :	black mound or hillside;
Banc Gelli-las :	hillside of green wood;
Banc Gwyn :	white hillside;
Banc Hir :	long hillside;
Banc Lluestnewydd :	hillside of the new hut;
Banc Myherin :	hillside of river Myherin;
Banc Ty-mawr :	hillside of the big house;
Banc y Defaid :	hillside of the sheep;
Bancyfelin :	hillside of the mill;
Banc y Gerlan :	hillside of the stream bank (or promenade);
Bangor :	wattled fence;
Banc Ystrad-wen :	hillside of the fair valley
Banwen :	moor of cotton-grass;
bedd :	a grave;
Beddau'r Cewri :	graves of the giants;
Beddgelert:	grave of Celert (pers. name): trad. grave of Celert, Prince Llewelyn's faithful hound
Beddugre :	grave of Ugre (pers. name);
Beguildy (Bugeildy) :	house of the shepherd;
Begwns :	beacons;
Beili :	yard; enclosure;
Beili Bedw Maen :	enclosure of birches (maen-stone);
Beili-brith :	mottled enclosure;
Beili Bychan :	little enclosure;
Benllech :	head of the rock;
Belan :	round-shaped hillock;
Berllan :	orchard;
Bermo, Y (Barmouth):	mouth of river Mawddach: (Abermawddach)
Berriew (Aber-rhiw) :	mouth of river Rhiw (slope);
berth (perth) :	a hedge or copse;
Berth-ddu :	black hedge;
Berth-fawr :	big hedge or copse;
Berth-las :	green hedge or copse;
Berwyn :	snowy summit;
Bethesda :	biblical name;
Betws :	house of prayer; oratory;
Betws Bledrws :	prayer house of Bledrws (pers. name);
Betws Diserth :	house of prayer in wilderness;
Betws Garmon :	prayer-house of Garmon;
Betws Gwerful Goch :	prayer house of Gwerful the Red;
Betws-y-coed ·	prayer house in the wood;
Betws-yn-Rhos :	prayer-house in Rhos (moorland);
Beudy-hir :	long cow-house;
blaen :	source of river; head of valley;
Blaenau :	plural of 'blaen';

Blaenau Ffestiniog :	valley heads of land of Ffestin;
Blaenannerch :	source of river Annerch (babbling);
Blaenbargod :	source of river Bargod (border river);
Blaen-bedw :	source of river Bedw (birches);
Blaencerniog :	source of river Cerniog (of cairns);
Blaen Coll :	source of river Coll (hazel trees);
Blaen Cowney :	source of river Cowney (of reeds);
Blaen-cwm :	head of valley;
Blaendyffryn :	head of valley;
Blaeneithon :	source of river Eithon (name of goddess);
Blaen-ffos :	source of ditch or brook;
Blaengeuffordd :	head of the road in hollow;
Blaen-glyn :	head of glen;
Blaen Henllan :	source of river Henllan (old church);
Blaen Hirnant :	source of river Hirnant (long stream);
Blaenllyndeg :	source of river Llyndeg (with pool);
Blaenmarlais :	source of river Marlais (march-horse, lais-ditch);
Blaen Peithnant :	source of river Peithnant;
Blaen-plwyf :	blaen—river source; plwyf—parish;
Blaen-porth :	blaen—river source; porth—harbour or gateway;
Blaentrinant :	prob. source of three streams;
Blaen Clawdd Ddu :	river source of the black hillside;
Blaen-y-pant :	head of the hollow;
Blaina (Blaenau) :	upper lands (stream sources);
Blawty :	flour house;
Bleddfa :	prob. (Bleddfach - pers. name);
Bodawen :	dwelling of the muse;
Bodelwyddan :	home of Elwyddan;
Bod-fach :	small dwelling;
Bodfari :	home of Fari?;
Bodfor :	big dwelling;
Bodnant (Bodnod) :	bod—home; nod—a feature;
Bodran :	a portion of land;
Bodtalog :	(uncertain) home of Talog; home of polluted water;
Boduan :	home of Buan (pers. name);
Bolbro :	protruding land; land of hollow;
Bolgoed :	trees of hollow; trees of protruding land;
Boncath :	prob. a buzzard;
Boncyn :	a mountain-side;
Boncyn Celyn :	mountainside of river Celyn (holly trees);
bont (pont) :	a bridge;
Bont Dolgadfan :	bridge of Cadfan's meadow;
Bont-ddu :	black bridge;
Bont Isa :	lower bridge;

Bontnewydd :	new bridge;
Bontrhydgaled :	bridge of the rough stream;
Borfa (porfa) :	a grazing place;
Borth :	a gateway or harbour;
Borth-wen :	fair gateway or harbour;
Borth-y-gest :	harbour of the cavity;
Botffordd :	house on the road;
Botwnnog :	home of Tywynnog;
Boughrood :	(uncertain) : bach—river bend; rhyd—ford;
Braich :	a promontory;
Braichyfedw :	promontory of birches (Bedw—river name);
Braich-y-waun :	promontory of the moorland;
Brechfa :	mottled place;
Brithdir :	mottled land;
Brithdir-coch :	red, mottled land;
Brochan :	a wild stream;
bron :	a hillside;
Bronafon :	hillside of a river;
Bron Ceiro :	hillside of river Ceiro (pers name);
Bronderw-goed :	hillside of oak-trees;
Bron-dre :	hillside of home or town;
Bronfelen :	brown or yellow hillside;
Bronhafod :	hillside of the summer-home;
Bron-haul :	hillside of the sun;
Bronheulwen :	hillside of sunshine;
Bronhyfryd :	pleasant hillside;
Broniarth :	hillside of enclosure or headland;
Bronllys (Brwynllys) :	court of rushes; (Brwyn—pers. name);
Bronant :	hillside of the stream or valley;
Bron Vyrnwy :	hillside of river Vyrnwy (Efyrnwy);
Bronwydd :	hillside of trees;
Bron-y-fedw :	hillside of birches (Bedw—river name);
Bron-y-Garn :	hillside of the cairn;
Bron y Garn-lwyd :	hillside of the grey cairn;
Bron-y-maen :	hillside of the rock;
Brwynen:	a river name (a rush);
Brychgoed :	mottled trees;
Brymbo (Bryn Baw) :	hill of dirt;
bryn :	a hill;
Brynaber :	hillside of river mouth;
Brynamlwg :	a clearly seen hill, or hill with clear view
Brynaman :	hill of river Aman;
Brynarian :	hill of silver;
Brynawelon :	hill of breezes;
Bryn-bach :	little hill;
Brynberian :	hill of Berian (pers. name);

Bryn Camlo :	hill of river Camlo (prob. pers name - crooked)
Bryncarnedd :	hill of the cairns;
Bryncastell :	hill of castle;
Bryn Cowney :	hill of river Cowney (reeds);
Bryn-cras :	dry or scorched hill;
Bryn-crug :	hill of the cairn;
Bryn Cyncoed :	hill of the chief or early wood;
Bryn Cynfelyn :	hill of Cynfelyn (pers. name);
Bryn Cyrch :	hill of oats or hill of river Cyrch;
Bryndadlau :	hill of assembly or of contention;
Brynderlwyn :	hill of oak-wood;
Bryn-derw :	hill of oak trees;
Brynderwen :	hill of oak tree;
Bryn Draenog :	hill of thorns;
Bryn-du :	black hill;
Bryn Ehedydd :	hill of lark;
Bryn Eithinog :	hill of gorse;
Bryn Garw :	a steep or rough hill;
Bryn-glas :	green hill;
Bryn-gwyn :	white hill;
Brynhelyg :	hill of willows;
Bryn-hir :	long hill;
Brynhyfryd :	pleasant hill;
Bryniau :	hills;
Brynllefrith :	hill of milk;
Brynllici :	hill of Lucy (pers. name);
Bryn Llysiau :	hill of herbs or grasses;
Brynllywarch :	hill of Llywarch (pers. name);
Bryn-mawr :	big hill;
Bryn Melys :	sweet hill;
Bryn Moel :	bare-topped hill;
Brynoerfa :	hill of cold spot;
Brynog :	hilly;
Bryn-oyre (oer) :	cold hill;
Bryn Penarth :	hill of headland;
Bryn Rhudd :	red hill;
Bryn Rhyg :	hill of rye;
Bryn Sadwrn :	hill of Sadwrn (pers. name);
Bryn Saith Marchog :	hill of the seven horsemen or knights
Brynsiencyn ::	hill of Siencyn;
Bryn Sych :	dry hill;
Bryn Tanat :	hill of river Tanat (shining water);
Bryn-teg :	fair hill;
Bryn Tegid :	hill of Tegid (pers. name);
Bryn Uchaf :	highest hill;
Bryn-wern :	hill of alder-wood or of marsh;
Bryn-y-brain :	hill of the crows;

14

Bryn y Castell :	hill of the castle;
Bryn-y-cil :	hill of the nook or river source;
Bryn y Fawnog :	hill of the peat-land;
Bryn y Fedwen :	hill of the birch-tree;
Bryn y Ffin :	hill of the boundary;
Bryn y Gadair :	hill of the fort (chair-shaped);
Bryn y Gof :	hill of the smith;
Bryn y Groes :	hill of the cross;
Bryn y Llys :	hill of the court;
Bryn y Maen :	hill of the rock;
Bryn-y-môr :	hill of the sea;
Bryn y Pentre :	hill of the village;
Bryn yr Wyn :	hill of the lambs;
Buarth :	a farm-yard; an enclosure;
Buches :	a cow pasture on hill;
Bugeilyn :	a sheep pasture;
Builth (Buallt) :	cow pasture;
Bwlch-bach :	little gap;
Bwlch Cae-haidd :	pass of the barley-field;
Bwlch-coch :	red pass;
Bwlch-coed :	pass of the trees;
Bwlch Coediog :	wooded pass;
Bwlch-gwyn :	white-pass;
Bwlchlluan (Bwlch y Lleian) :	pass of the nun;
Bwlch-mawr :	big pass;
Bwlch-sych :	dry pass;
Bwlchtocyn :	pass of the hill;
Bwlch y Cilau :	pass of river sources or of nooks;
Bwlch y Grogfa :	pass of the gallows;
Bwlch y Ddâr :	pass of the oaks;
Bwlch y Ddau Faen :	pass of the two stones;
Bwlch y Ddwy Allt :	pass of the two slopes or woods;
Bwlch y Fan :	pass of the peak;
Bwlchyfedwen :	pass of the birch-tree;
Bwlch y Ffridd :	pass of the mountain-pasture;
Bwlch y Garreg :	pass of the rock;
Bwlch y Graig :	pass of the rock;
Bwlch y Llan :	pass of the church or village;
Bwlch y Llyn :	pass of the lake;
Bwlch y Mynydd :	mountain pass;
Bwlch yr Adwy Wynt :	pass of the wind-gap;
Bwthyn :	cottage;
Dylchau :	passes or gaps;
Byrlymau Elan :	rapids or bubbles of river Elan;
Cabalfa :	place of the ferry;
Caban-coch :	red cabin;

Cadnant :	boss. brook connected with a battle;
caeau :	fields;
Caeauduon :	black fields
Cae-crwn :	round field
Cae Gaer :	field of fort or camp
Cae-garw :	rough field
Cae Heylin :	field of Heylin (pers. name)
Caehopcyn :	field of Hopcyn (pers. name)
Caeliber :	cottage field
Cae Lluest :	field of hut (shepherd's cabin)
Cae Mawr :	big field
Cae Melyn :	brown or yellow field
Caeo :	(uncertain): a pers. name; from 'cau'—to enclose
Caepandy :	field of the fulling-mill
Caeprior :	field of the prior
Caer Beris :	fort of Beris (pers. name)
Cae'r Bwla :	field of the bull
Caer Capan :	fort on hill-top or (Cae'r—field of)
Caer Din :	enclosed fort
Caer Du :	black fort
Caereinion :	fort of Einion (pers. name)
Cae'r Eithin :	gorse field
Caer Fadog :	fort of Madog
Caer Fagu (Gardd Fagu) :	land of Fagu (pers. name)
Caerfyrddin (Carmarthen):	fort of Morddin or fort by the sea. Also believed to be the fort of Merlin the sorcerer, Myrddin being Welsh for Merlin
Cae'r-gôg :	field of the cuckoo
Cae'r Gweision :	field of the servants
Caergwrle :	fort of Gwrle;
Caergybi (Holyhead) :	fort of Cybi (pers. name);
Cae'r-lan :	field of the river-bank
Caernarvon :	fort near Môn (Anglesey);
Cae'r Neuadd :	field of the hall
Caer Noddfa :	fort of refuge
Caer-sws :	fort of Sws (pers. name)
Callwen :	a pers. name
Camddwr :	a winding stream (name of river)
Camlo :	a winding stream (from pers. name)
Cammen Ucha;	a winding stream (from pers. name)
Camnant :	a winding stream
Canol-maes :	middle of meadow
Cantref:	an ancient land area of 100 homesteads
capel :	a chapel
Capel Bangor :	capel—chapel; Bangor—wattled fence
Capel Betws Lleucu :	prayer-house of Lleucu (pers. name)
Capel Celyn :	chapel of river Celyn (holly)
Capel Curig :	the chapel of Curig

Capel Dewi :	chapel of David (St. David)
Capel Ffraid :	chapel of St. Bridget
Capel Garmon :	the chapel of Garmon
Capel Issac :	chapel of Isaac
Capel Seion :	chapel of Zion
Capel-y-ffin :	chapel of boundary
Capel y Wig :	chapel of the wood
Cardigan (Ceredigion) :	the land of Ceredig (pers. name)
carn :	heap of stones; a cairn
Carnau Cefn y Ffordd :	cairns of the ridge-way
Carneddau :	cairns
Carnedd Ddafydd :	the cairn of Dafydd
Carnedd Illog :	cairn of Illog (pers. name)
Carnedd Llywelyn :	the cairn of Llywelyn
Carnedd-wen :	white cairn
Carn Hyddgen :	cairn of Hyddgen (pers. name)
Carn Nant-y-ffordd :	cairn of the road valley
Carno :	place of cairns
Carn Pant Maen-llwyd :	cairn of hollow of grey stone
Carn y Geifr :	cairn of the goats
carreg :	a rock
Carregbica :	pointed rock
Carreg Cennen :	rock of river Cennen (pers. name)
Carreg Hwfa :	rock of Hwfa (pers. name)
Carreg Sawdde :	rock of river Sawdde (from suddo—to sink)
Carreg-wen :	white rock
Carregwiber :	rock of the viper
Carreg y Big :	rock of the peak
Carrog :	swift-flowing stream
Cartref :	home
castell :	a castle
Castell Cae Maerdy :	castle of the field of the steward's house
Castell Caereinion :	castle of Einion's fort
Castell Collen :	castle of Collen (pers. name) or hazel trees
Castell Dolforwyn :	castle of the maid's meadow
Castell-du :	black castle
Castell Foel Allt :	castle of the bare hillside
Castell Hywel :	Hywel's castle
Castell Moch :	castle of the pigs
Castellnewydd Emlyn :	new castle in Emlyn (a territory)
Castell Powys :	castle of Powys (an ancient territory)
Castell Tomen-y-mur :	castle of the mound of the wall
Castell y Blaidd :	castle of the wolf
Castell y Garn :	castle of the cairn
Cathedin :	prob. land of Cathed (pers. name)
Cawell y Cimwch :	the lobster-pot
cefnau :	hillside or ridge
Cefn :	ridges

Cefn aelwyd—hearth
bach—small
blaen—source
blewog—grassy
boeth—hot
brith—mottled
brwyn—rushes
brwynog—of rushes
Brynich—pers.name
bychan—small
carnedd—cairns
castell—castle
cenarth—of lichen
coch—red
craig—rock
crin—dry
dre—town
dyrys—difficult
eryri—highlands
faes—meadow
fron—hillside
garw—rough
glas—green; blue
golau—light

gorwydd—big wood
gribin—crest
grug—heather
grugos—of heather
gwernfa—marsh
gwyn—white
hafod—summer home
hendre—old home
hir—long
hirbrisg—long brushwood
llan—church, parish
llwyd—grey
llwyni—bushes
llydan—wide
llys—court
maes—meadow
mawr—big
parc—park
penarth—promontory
perfedd—middle land
rhydoldog—winding brook
tre yspyty—home of hospice
twlch—hut, cottage

Cefn Cantref :	cefn-ridge; cantref—ancient land area
Cefncoedycymer :	wooded ridge of river confluence
Cefnddwysarn :	the ridge of the two paved ways
Cefn Melindwr :	ridge of river Melindwr (water-mill)
Cefn-y-bedd :	ridge of the grave
Cegidfa :	place of hemlock
Cegin Fach :	little kitchen
Ceinewydd :	new quay
Celynog :	place of holly
Cellan :	a small cell
Cemais :	river bend
Ceredigion :	land of Ceredig (pers. name)
Cerniau :	place of cairns
cerrig :	stones
Cerrigceinwen :	rocks of Ceinwen (pers. name)
Cerrigcochion :	red stones
Cerrig Cyplau :	coupling stones
Cerrig Gwalch :	rocks of the hawk
Cerrig Gwaun y Llan :	rocks of the church meadow
Cerrigwynion :	white stones
Cerrig-y-cwm :	stones of the valley
Cerrigydrudion :	crag of the warriors
Cerrig yr Wyn :	rocks of the lambs
cil :	a nook; source of stream
Chwilog :	place of beetles
Cilcain :	pleasant nook
Cilcennin :	source of river Cennin (pers. name)

Cileos :	nook of nightingale
Cilfach-allt :	nook of hillside or wood
Cilfodig :	nook of small dwelling
Cilfor :	large nook
Cilgwyn :	white nook or source
Cil-haul :	prob. shelter from sun
Ciliau :	plural of cil (nooks) (sources)
Ciliau Aeron :	nooks or bends of river Aeron (a goddess)
Cilie :	nooks
Cilmeri :	recess of brambles
Ciloerwynt :	poss. shelter from cold wind
Cil-rhew :	nook or source of ice or frost
Cil-y-cwm :	river source of valley
Cil-yr-ych :	recess of the oxen
Cim :	1. pers. name; 2. border of common
Cistfaen :	a sepulchre
Claerwen :	bright, shining water
Clarach :	flat land
Clas :	a religious community
Clawdd :	bank; hedge; hillside; ditch
Clawdd-coch :	red hillside
Clawdd Du Bach :	little, black hillside
Clawdd Mawr :	big hillside
Clawdd y Coed :	hillside of the trees
Clegyr Nant :	rocky stream or valley
Cletwr :	hard, rough water
Clipiau :	steep hillsides
Clocaenog :	clôg (knoll); caenog (of lichen)
Cloch-fach :	stream with sound as of a bell
Clochnant :	stream with sound as of a bell
Cloddiau :	banks or ditches
Clogau :	knolls, crags or cliffs
Clogwyn :	a crag or cliff
Clunderwen :	meadow of the oak tree
Clwt-y-bont :	plot of land of bridge
Clwyd :	a hurdle
Clydach :	a rocky stream
Clyne (Y Clun) :	the meadow
Clynnog :	place of holly
Clyro (Cleirwy) :	shining water; Gwy—river Wye?
Clywedog :	river name (heard from afar)
Cnapiau'r Ferlen :	mounds of the pony
Cnewr :	prob. Cyniwair—meandering stream
Cnicht, y :	from the English word 'knight'
Cnwch :	a small tump
Coedcae :	land with small trees, usually at bottom of mountain
Coed Celli :	wood of hazel-trees

Coedgenau :	trees at the opening or jaws
Coed Glason :	wood of river Glason (blue, green water)
Coed Llawr-y-cwm :	wood at bottom of valley
Coed Llynlloedd :	wood of stagnant pool
Coed Mawr :	big wood
Coed Owen :	wood of Owen
Coed-poeth :	hot wood (burnt)
Coed Rhos :	wood of moorland
Coed-tew :	thick wood
Coedtrefle :	wood of the dwelling
Coed y Ban :	wood of the peak
Coed-y-bryn :	wood of the hill
Coed y Cwm :	wood of the valley
Coed y Dinas :	wood of the fort
Coed y Gaer :	wood of the fort
Coed y Llan :	wood of the church or parish
Coed y Maen :	wood of the rock
Coed y Marchog :	wood of the knight or horseman
Coed yr Ystrad :	wood of the vale
Coed y Wlad :	wood of the district
Coegen :	stream that dries : empty
Coelbren, Y :	the ballot-stick
Coetmor :	large wood
Coity (Coed, ty) :	house in wood
Colfa :	mountain pass; a branch or bough
Collfryn :	river name; hill of hazel-trees
Colwyn :	a young dog
Commins-coch :	red commons
Commins-bach :	little commons
Commins Uchaf :	upper commons
Commin y Garth :	common of the headland
Conwy :	name of river (full and flowing)
copa :	summit
Corngafallt :	corn-peak; gafallt—poss. name of King Arthur's dog
Corun y Ffridd :	top of the mountain-pasture
Corwen (Corfaen) :	stone denoting a sacred spot
Craig :	rock or crag

cribyn—crest	nant—stream, glen
Cwm Clyd—sheltered valley	pwll du—black pool
ddu—black	safn-y-coed—wood opening
fawr—big	y Deryn—of the bird
foel—bare	y Dderwen—of the oak
for—big	y maes—of the field
fryn—hill	y march—of the horse
fuddai—milk churn	y nos—of the night
Garth Bwlch—headland pass	y pant—of the hollow
Gellidywyll—dark wood	y pistyll—of the spring
le—place	yr allt goch—of the red slope
lluest—cabin, hut	yr ogof—of the cave

Cray (Crai) :	fresh, raw water
Cregrina (Craig Furuna) :	rock of Furuna (pers. name)
Creigiau :	rocks, cliff
Creigiaullwydion :	grey rocks
Creignant :	stream of the rocks
Cribarth :	crest of mountain; ridge headland
Cribyn :	a crest
Cribyn-llwyd :	grey crest
Cricieth :	crug (cairn); caith (confined)
Crickadarn (Crucadarn) :	strong mound or cairn
Crickhowell (Crucywel) :	mound of Howell
Criggion (Crugyn) :	small mound or cairn
Crinfynydd :	dry mountain (or cryn—round)
Cringoed :	dry wood (or round wood)
Cripiau Eisteddfa-fach :	slopes of resting-place; fach—small
Crochan :	a pot or cauldron
Croes :	a cross; crossroad
Croes-faen :	stone cross
Croesty :	house at crossroads
Crofty :	house of little field
Crogau :	gallows; crucifixes
Croniarth :	round enclousre or headland
Crug :	a mound; cairn; heap of stones on hill
Crugion :	mounds; cairns
Crug-y-bar :	cairn of the peak
Crugyn :	a small cairn or mound
Crugyn Gwyddel :	mound of trees (or Irishman)
Crugyn Rhyd :	mound of the ford or brook
Crug yr Wyn :	mound of the lambs
Crwbin :	a mound
Crygnant :	valley or brook of the mound
Cutiau :	huts
Cwm :	a shallow valley (bowl-shaped)

afon—river	gwŷdd—wood
Ann—pers. name	gwyn—white; fair
Anod—river name	Hawen—river name
bach—small	hir—long
belan—round hill	Hirnant—river name (long)
berllan—orchard	Ifor—pers. name
biga—peak	lladron—robbers
brain—cows	llech—river name (stone)
brith—mottled	llechwedd—hillside
bugail—shepherd	Llinau—river name
bustach—steer	maerdy—steward's house
byr—short	mawr—big
cae—field	meichiad—swineherd
calch—lime	nant—brook; valley
cefn y gaer—ridge fort	nant-gwyn: white brook
Cewydd—pers. name	nanty (nantau): brooks
craig—rock	nantygelli : stream of the wood

Cynfelyn—pers. name
derw—oaks
du—black
Duad—river name
Dulas—river name
dŵr—water
dwrgi—otter
dylluan—owl
ffalde—folds
fforest—moorland
ffridd—hill pasture
ffrwd—stream
ffynnon—well
Gwdi—river name

Nant-y-moch: Stream of the pigs
Tawe: river name (quiet; bend)
Tudu—pers. name
Twrch—river name (burrowing)
Rheidol—river name
rhiwdre—hillside home
Saeson—Englishmen
Wysg—river name (fish)
y-bont—of the bridge
ychen—oxen
y-fron—of the hillside
ysgawen—elder tree
Ystwyth—river name (meandering)

Cwm-bach Llechryd :	little valley of brook with stony bed
Cwmcamlais :	valley of river Camlais (winding)
Cwmdeuddwr (Cwmwd Deuddwr) :	cwmwd—ancient division of land deuddwr—two rivers
Cwm Pennant :	cwm-valley; pennant - end of brook or valley
Cwmwr Uchaf :	an embankment (uchaf—upper)
Cwm-y-glo :	valley of the coal
Cwrt :	a court or mansion
Cwrt Llechryd :	court of river Llechryd (stony bed)
Cwrtnewydd :	new court
Cwrtycadno :	court of the fox
Cwrt y Person :	court of the clergyman
Cyfarthfa :	place of barking (dogs or foxes)
Cyfronnydd :	hillside fields
Cyffiau :	borders
Cyffin-fawr :	border (fawr—big)
Cynghordy :	house of meeting or assembly (or cynhordy—a lodge)
Cynhinfa (Cenninfa) :	place of leeks
Cynwyd :	(pers. name)
dan :	below, under
Dan-y-coed :	below the wood
Danyderi :	below the oak trees
Dan-y-graig :	below the rock
Danymyarth :	below the cattle enclosure
Danyreglwys :	below the church
Danyrepynt :	below the Epynt mountain
Danyrogof :	below the cave
Darowen :	Owen's oaks
Darren :	a rocky hillside; a precipice
Darrenfelen :	brown or yellow rocky hillside
Das Eithin :	gorse mound
Defynnog :	poss. from pers. name

22

Degannwy :	land of Decanae tribe
Deildre :	leafy home
Derlwyn :	oak grove
Dernol :	prob. a personal name
Derwen :	an oak tree
Derwen-gam :	crooked oak
Derwen-las :	green oak
Derwllwydion :	grey oaks
Derwydd :	oak grove
Deuddwr :	two waters
Deythur (Deuddwr) :	two waters
Diffwys :	wilderness; steep slope
Dihewyd :	a pleasant place
Dinas :	a fort or camp
Dinbych (Denbigh) :	little fort
Dinllan :	din—fort; llan—church
Dinlleu :	fort of Lleu (pers. name)
Dinmel :	fort of a prince
Dinnant :	din—fort; nant—stream or valley
Diosg :	a woody place
Disgwylfa :	a watching place
Diserth :	wilderness; retreat
dôl :	a meadow; a river meadow
Doladron :	robbers' meadow
Dolafallen :	meadow of apple tree
Dolanog :	winding with meadows on bank
Dolarddyn :	meadow of Arddyn (pers. name)
Dolau :	meadows
Dolau Cothi :	meadows of river Cothi (swift)
Dolau Hirion :	long meadows
Dolbadarn :	meadow of Padarn (pers. name)
Dolben-maen :	meadow at head of rock
Dôl-bryn :	meadow of the hill
Doldowlod :	meadow of the hay-loft
Dôl-fach :	little meadow
Dôl-fawr :	big meadow
Dolfelin :	mill meadow
Dolfor :	big meadow
Dolforwyn :	prob. meadow of maid
Dolfriog :	meadow of the high land; brambles
Dolgadfan :	meadow of Cadfan (pers. name)
Dolgarrog :	meadow of swift-flowing stream
Dôl-gau :	meadow of hollow
Dolgarnedd :	meadow of the cairns
Dolgellau :	meadow of the monks' cells
Dôl-goch :	red meadow
Dôl-goed :	meadow of the wood
Dôl Gownwy :	meadow of the river Cownwy (reeds)

23

Dolgwden :	meadow of river Gwden (willow shoots)
Dolgwenith :	meadow of wheat
Dôl-gwyn Felin :	white meadow of mill
Dôl Hafren :	meadow of river Severn
Dolhelfa :	hunting meadow
Dôl-las :	green meadow
Dôl Llugan :	meadow of river Llugan (shining)
Dôl Llwyn-hir :	meadow of long wood
Dolmenyn :	butter meadow
Dolpebyll :	meadow of the tents
Dôl-rhiw :	meadow of the hillside
Dolwar-fach :	(uncertain) dôl—meadow; war—above; fach—small
Dôl-wen :	fair meadow
Dolwyddelan :	meadow of Wyddelan (pers. name)
Dôl-y-bont :	meadow of the bridge
Dôl-y-coed :	meadow of the wood
Dôl-y-dre :	meadow of the homestead
Dolyfelin :	meadow of the mill
Dôl-y-gaer :	meadow of the cairn
Dôl y Garreg-wen :	meadow of the white rock
Dôl y Gaseg :	meadow of the mare
Dolau-hir :	long meadows
Dôl-y-maen :	meadow of the rock
Dolypandy :	meadow of the fulling-mill
Dolaumelinau :	meadows of the mills
Dôl y Mynach :	meadow of the monk
Dolyrerw :	meadow of the acre
Dolyronnen :	meadow of the ash-tree
Domen-ddu :	black mound
Domen Gastell :	castle of the mound
Domen yr Allt :	mound of the hillside
Dorlan-goch :	red river-bank
Draenllwyn :	thornbush
Drain :	thorns
Draws Drum :	cross ridge
Dre-fach :	little home
Drefor :	big home
Drevour (Dre-fawr) :	big homestead
Drosgl, y :	the hard, rough place
Drum :	a ridge or summit
Drum Ddu :	black ridge
Drum Maen :	ridge of the rock
Drws-y-Coed :	opening of the woods
Drws-y-nant :	opening of the stream
Drysgol :	a rough place
Dryslwyn :	thornbush or brambles
Dugoedydd :	black woods

Dwyfor :	larger Dwy river, named after a goddess
Dwygyfylchi :	round forts; dwy = two
Dwyryd :	two fords or streams
Dyfed :	name of old tribal land
Dyfnant :	deep stream or valley
Dyffryn :	a valley
Dyffryn Castell :	valley of river Castell (Castle)
Dyffryn Ceidrych :	valley of river Ceidrych (pers, name)
Dyffryn Crawnon :	valley of river Crawnon
Dyffryn Dulas :	valley of river Dulas (dark)
Dyffryn Tanad :	valley of river Tanad (shining)
Dylife :	floods
Dynefwr :	din—fort; efwr—cow parsnip
Dysserth (Diserth) :	a wilderness
Dderw :	oak trees
Ddôl :	a meadow (near river)
Dduallt :	black hillside
Edwinsford (Rhydodyn) :	ford of lime-kiln
Efail-fach :	little smithy
Efail-rhyd :	smithy of the ford or stream
Efail-wen :	fair smithy
Efailnewydd :	new smithy
Efenechtyd :	a monastery
eglwys :	church
Eglwys-fach :	little church
Eglwyswrw :	church of Wrw (pers, name)
Eisteddfa Gurig :	resting place of Curig (pers. name)
Eithinog :	place of gorse
Elan :	river name (pers. name)
Elerch :	river name (pers. name)
Elidir :	a pers. name
Epynt :	haunt of the pony
Erddig :	a garden
Erw :	an acre; a plot of land
Erwbeudy :	acre of the cow-house
Erw-ddôl :	meadow of the acre
Erw Glanyrafon :	acre of the river bank
Erw-goch :	red acre
Erw-lôn :	acre of the lane
Eryri :	high land
esgair :	a mountain ridge
Esgair Clawdd :	ridge of the mountain bank
Esgair Cywion :	ridge of the young animals
Esgairdraenllwyn :	ridge of the thornbush
Esgair Dderwen :	ridge of the oak-tree
Esgair-ddu :	black ridge
Esgair Elan :	ridge of the river Elan (pers. name)

Esgair Fawr :	big ridge
Esgair Fraith :	mottled ridge
Esgairganol :	middle ridge
Esgair Garthen :	ridge of small headland
Esgair Geiliog :	prob. ridge of Cyfeiliog (pers. name)
Esgair Gelynen :	ridge of holly (stream name)
Esgair Geulan :	ridge of hollow river bank
Esgair-gul :	narrow ridge
Esgair Llwyn-gwyn :	ridge of the white bush
Esgair Llys :	ridge of the court
Esgair Maen :	ridge of the rock
Esgair Meini Gwynion :	ridge of the white rocks
Esgair Moel :	ridge of bare hill
Esgair Nantau :	ridge of the streams
Esgair Pentre-mawr :	ridge of the large village
Esgair Penygarreg :	ridge of the head of the rock
Esgair Perfedd :	ridge of the middle land
Esgair Priciau :	ridge of the sticks (bushes)
Esgairwy :	ridge of river Wye
Esgair Ychain :	ridge of the oxen
Esgair y Ffynnon :	ridge of the well
Esgair y Gader :	ridge of the fort
Esgair y Graig :	ridge of the rock
Esgair y Maes :	ridge of the meadow
Esgair y Maesnant :	ridge of the meadow stream
Esgair y Tŷ :	ridge of the house
Fach :	a nook or a bend in a river
Fach-wen :	fair nook
Faenor Uchaf :	upper manor (chief's home of stone)
Faerdre :	steward's house
Fagwyr :	a rocky place; walls
Fainc-ddu :	black bench (or ledge)
Fan Bwlch Chwyth :	peak of windy pass
Fan Llia :	peak of river Llia
Fawnog :	place of peat
Fawnog Figyn :	peat bog
fedw :	birch trees
Fedw-ddu :	black birches
Fedw-lwyd :	grey birches
Feidr :	a lane
Felindre :	home of mill; home of the villeins
Felin-fach :	little mill
Felin-ganol :	middle mill
Felin-gwm :	valley of the mill
Felinnewydd :	new mill
Felin-wen :	white mill
Felin-wynt :	windmill

Fign Aberbiga :	bog at mouth of river Biga (peak)
Foel :	a bare-topped hill
Foel Fawr :	big bare hill
Foel Gurig :	bare hill of Curig (pers. name)
Foel Rhudd :	red, bare hill
Foel Wen :	the white or fair bare-topped hill
Foel Wyddon :	bare hill-top of the witch (poss. pers. name)
Friog :	place of brambles; high land
Fron :	a hillside
Froncysyllte :	hillside of the joining
Fronddyrys :	a difficult slope
Fron-goch :	red slope
Fron-haul :	hillside of the sun
Fronheulog :	sunny hillside
Fron-wen :	white hillside
Fuches :	a cow pasture or fold
Fuches-gau :	enclosed cow-pasture
Fuches-wen :	white cow-pasture
Ffair-fach :	ffair—fair; fach—small
Ffair-rhos :	fair of the moorland
Ffald y Brenin :	the king's pound
Ffawyddog :	place of beech-trees
Ffestiniog :	land of Ffestin (pers. name)
Ffinnant :	border stream
Ffordd-fawr :	main road
Ffordd-gefn :	road over hillside (ridgeway)
Ffordd-las :	green road
Fforest :	moorland
Ffos :	a ditch or brook
Ffos-y-ffin :	ditch of the border
Ffridd :	mountain pasture
Ffridd Braich-llwyd	pasture of grey spur
Ffridd Bryn Gogledd :	pasture of northern hill
Ffridd Cae Pen-ffos :	pasture of field at head of ditch
Ffridd Dôl-y-maen :	pasture of meadow of the rock
Ffridd-fach :	little mountain pasture
Ffridd Faldwyn :	pasture of Maldwyn (Baldwin)
Ffridd-fawr :	big mountain pasture
Ffridd Ganol :	middle mountain pasture
Ffridd Goch :	red mountain pasture
Ffriddisaf :	lower mountain pasture
Ffridd Llannerch :	mountain pasture of the glade
Ffridd Llwydiarth :	pasture of the grey headland
Ffridd Mathrafal :	pasture where two rivers meet— a triangle
Ffridd Rhosygarreg :	pasture of the moor of the rock
Ffridd Wyllt :	wild mountain pasture
Ffrwd :	a stream

Ffrwd-grech :	rippling stream
Ffrwd-wen :	white stream
Ffynhonnau :	wells or springs
Ffynnon :	a well or spring
Ffynnon Arthur :	Arthur's well
Ffynnon-bedr :	St. Peter's well
Ffynnon Dewi :	St. David's well
Ffynnon Garmon :	well of Garmon (pers. name)
Ffynnon Garreg :	well of rock
Ffynnongroyw :	fresh, clear well
Ffynnon Gynydd (Ffynnon Gynidr) :	well of St. Cynidr
Ffynnon Illog :	well of Illog (pers. name)
Ffynnon-oer :	cold well
Ffynnon-wen :	white, holy, or fair well
Gaer :	a fort or camp
Gallt :	a wood or hillside
Gallt yr Ancr :	wood of the hermit
Gamallt :	winding hill road
Gamriw :	winding ascent
Garthen :	hillside or enclosure
Garth-gell :	enclosure of Cell (pers. name)
Garn :	a heap of stones or cairn
Garnant :	rough stream
Garn Bryn-llwyd :	cairn of the grey hill
Garn-fach Bugeilyn :	little cairn of shepherd's pasture
Garn-wen :	white cairn
Garreg :	a rock or cliff
Garreg Ddu :	black rock
Garreg Felen :	yellow rock (or brown)
Garreg-hir :	long rock or cliff
Garreg-lwyd :	grey rock
Garreg y Gwynt :	rock of the wind
Garth :	headland of enclosure
Garthangharad :	headland or enclosure of Angharad
Garthbeibio :	enclosure of Beibio (pers. name)
Garthbrengi :	enclosure or headland of Brengi (pers. name)
Garth Eryr :	headland of the eagle
Garth Heilyn :	enclosure of Heilyn (pers. name)
Gaufron :	enclosed hillside
Geifr :	goats
Gelynnen :	a holly tree
Gelli :	a small wood
Gelliau :	cells
Gelli-aur :	golden grove
Gellidywyll :	dark wood

Gelli Faenog :	wood of the rocky place
Gelli-fawr :	big wood
Gelli-fudr :	polluted wood
Gelli-garn :	wood of the cairn
Gelli-goch :	red wood
Gelli-hir :	long wood
Gellilefrith :	milk wood
Gelli-wen :	fair wood
Gerddigleision :	green gardens
Ger y Tarell :	near river Tarell
Gesail Ddu :	black nook of mountain
Geseilfa :	place of mountain recess
Geufron :	an enclosed hillside
Geuffordd :	road in hollow
Gilfach :	small recess
Gilfach yr Halen :	recess of the salt water
Gilfach yr Heol :	recess of the road
Gilfach y Rhiw :	recess of the hillside
Gilwern :	recess of marsh or alders
Glan :	a river bank
Glanbechan :	bank of river Bechan (small)
Glanbrydan :	bank of river Brydan (warm water)
Glan Ceirw (Glan Eirw) :	rippling foam
Glanduar :	bank of river Duar
Glandulas :	bank of river Dulas (dark water)
Glan-dŵr :	river bank
Glandyfi :	bank of river Dyfi (black water)
Glanfedwen :	bank of river Bedwen (birch)
Glanfrogan :	bank of river Brogan (slow and winding)
Glangrwyne :	bank of river Grwyne
Glan Gwy :	bank of river Wye
Glangwydderig :	bank of river Gwydderig
Glanhafon :	bank of river Hafon
Glanhanog :	bank of river Hanog
Glan Hafren :	bank of river Hafren (slow-flowing)
Glan Ithon :	bank of river Ithon (name of a goddess)
Glaniwrch :	bank of river Iwrch (stag)
Glan-llyn :	bank of lake
Glanmiheli :	bank of river Miheli (prob. Heli— pers. name)
Glan Mule :	bank of river Miwl
Glannau :	river banks
Glan-oer :	cold banks
Glan-rhos :	moorland bank
Glan-rhyd :	bank of stream
Glansefin (Llansefin) :	church or place of Sefin (pers. name)

29

Glansevern :	bank of river Severn
Glan Vyrnwy :	bank of river Efyrnwy
Glan-wern :	bank of marsh
Glan-y-môr :	sea-shore
Glan-y-nant :	bank of the stream
Glanymynech :	bank of river Mynech
Glasbury (Clas ar Wy) :	religious community on the Wye
Glasfynydd :	green mountain
Glasgoed :	green wood
Glasgwm :	green valley
Glaslyn :	blue or green lake or valley
Glasnant :	blue or green valley or stream
Gliffaes (Gwlith-faes) :	dewy meadow
Glôg :	a knoll; a rock
Gludair, y :	the heap of stones
Glyn :	a glen
Glynceiriog :	valley of river Ceiriog (loved, friendly)
Glyndyfrdwy :	glen of river Dyfrdwy (water; a goddess)
Glyn Feirion :	glen of Meirion (pers. name)
Glyn Gwy :	glen of river Wye
Glynhafren :	glen of river Severn
Glyntrefnant :	glen of homestead stream
Glyntwymyn :	glen of river Twymyn (warm)
Goetre (Coed-tre) :	home in wood
Gogarth :	a low rise in ground
Gogerddan :	a step or rise
Goginan :	from 'cegin', obsolete word for mountain ridge
Golan :	a biblical place
Gorddwr :	river source; flood
Gorlan :	a fold
Gorllwyn :	large wood
gors :	a marsh
Gorseinon :	marsh of Einon (pers. name)
Gors-goch :	red marsh
Gors Gwndwn :	marsh of fallow-land
Gorslydan :	wide marsh
Goytre (Coed-tre) :	house in wood
graig :	a rock or crag
Graig-fawr :	big crag
Graig-goch :	red rock
Graig yr Onnen :	rock of the ash-tree
Gregynog :	prob. place of heather
Gribin :	mountain crest
Gro :	pebbles or gravel
Groes :	cross or crossroad
Grosffordd :	crossroad
Groeslon, y :	the cross lane
Groes y Forwyn :	cross of the maid

Gronant :	pebbly stream; round valley
grug :	heather
Gruglwyn :	heather bush
Gwaelod :	bottom land
Gwaelod y Rhos :	moorland bottom
Gwaith Goginan :	Goginan mine
Gwaunydd :	moors or meadows
Gwalchmai :	a pers. name
Gwarallt :	nape of hillside or wood
Gwar-y-tŷ :	above the house
Gwastad :	flat land
Gwastad-y-coed :	flat land of wood
gwaun :	a meadow
Gwaun Ceste :	meadow or moor of river Ceste
Gwaun Tre Beddau :	moor of the home of graves
Gwaunynog (Gwenynog) :	place of bees
Gwaunysgor :	meadow of the camp
Gwely Gwyddfarch :	land of Gwyddfarch (pers. name)
Gwely Melangell :	land of Melangell (pers. name)
Gwenddwr :	fair water
Gwenfron :	fair or white hillside
gwern :	marsh or alder trees
Gwernafon :	river of marsh or alders
Gwern Allt y Cwm :	marsh of hillside of valley
Gwernamlwg :	prominent alders or marsh
Gwernesgob :	marsh of the bishop
Gwern-ffridd :	marsh or alders of mountain pasture
Gwern Pen-y-nant :	marsh of head of valley or stream
Gwernybuarth :	marsh of farmyard or cow-pasture
Gwern-y-bwlch :	marsh of the pass
Gwernydd :	marshes or alders
Gwernyfed :	poss. sacred glade in alders
Gwern y Geufron :	marsh of enclosed hillside
Gwern-y-go:	marsh of the smith
Gwernymynydd :	marsh of the mountain
Gwern-y-pwll :	marsh of the pit or pool
Gwydyr (Gwydir) :	low land
Gwyddelwern :	marsh of the Irishman (or alders)
Gwyddgrug :	grave of stones
gwyn :	white; fair; blessed
Gwynfaen :	white stone
Gwynfe :	white or fair plain
Gwynfynydd :	white mountain
Gwynedd ·	land of the Venedotae (tribe)
Gwytherin :	a personal name
Gwyrfai :	a winding stream
Gyffyliog :	a tree stump
Gyfylchi :	round fort

Gyrn Goch :	red cairns
Gyrn Moelfre :	cairns of the bare mountain
Gyrnos :	place of cairns
Hafan :	haven
Hafod :	summer dwelling and pasture
Hafod Fraith :	mottled summer pasture
Hafod-fudr :	polluted summer pasture
Hafod-lom :	poor summer pasture or dwelling
Hafodlydan :	wide summer house or pasture
Hafod-wen :	fair summer pasture or dwelling
Hafod y Beudy :	summer house of the cow-house
Hafodygarreg :	summer house of the rock
Hafoty Cedig :	summer house of Cedig (pers. name)
Hafren :	Severn river
Halkyn (Helygen) :	willow tree
Harlech :	beautiful rock
Helyg :	willow trees
Hen Allt :	old wood or hillside
Henblas :	old mansion
Hen-bwll :	old pit or pool
Hen-dai :	old houses
Hen Domen :	old mound
Hendre :	winter dwelling (main home)
Hendre Einon :	winter home of Einon
Hendre-hen :	old winter home
Hendwr :	old water
Hendy :	old house
Hendy-gwyn (Whitland) :	old, white house
Hen Efail :	old smithy
Henfron :	old hillside
Henfaes :	old meadow
Hen-gefn :	old ridge
Hen Gerrig :	old rocks
Hengoed :	old wood
Hengwm :	old valley
Hengwm Cyfeiliog :	old valley of Cyfeiliog (pers. name)
Henhafod :	old summer home
Heniarth :	old headland or enclosure
Henllan :	old church
Henryd :	old ford
Hen Rhyd-fawr :	old ford; fawr—big
heol :	a road
Heolgaled :	difficult road (or rough)
Heol-las :	green road
Heol Sant Catwg :	road of St. Catwg
Heolsenni :	road of river Senni (prob. pers. name)
Heol-y-gaer :	road of the fort

Hepste :	a river that dries up
Hirael (Hir Erw) :	long acre :
Hirddu :	stream name (long and black)
Hirllwyn :	long wood or brush
Hirnant :	long stream
Hir Rhos :	long moorland
Hir Rhyd :	long stream or ford
Hirwaun :	long meadow or moorland
Howey (Hywi) :	name of river
Kinmel (Cinmel) :	the retreat of Mael (pers. name)
lan :	ascent
Lan-goch :	red slope
Libanus (Lebanon) :	biblical place
Login :	from 'halog'—polluted
Llaethdy :	a dairy
llan :	orig. an enclosure, now 'church'. Usually followed by name of saint, though spelling is uncertain :—

Llanafan	Llanddeiniol	Llangollen
Llananno	Llandderfel	Llangrannog
Llanarthney	Llanddona	Llangunllo
Llanasa	Llanddwyn	Llangwyfan
Llanbabo	Llanelwedd	Llangynidr
Llanbadarn	Llanelli	Llangynin
Llanbaylow	Llanenddwyn	Llangynnyr
Llan-bedr	Llanengan	Llangynog
Llanbeilin	Llanerfyl	Llangynyw
Llanbister	Llanfachreth	Llanhaylow
Llandanwg	Llanfadoc	Llanidloes
Llandecwyn	Llan-fair	Llanigon
Llandefaelog	Llanfallteg	Llanilar
Llandegley	Llanfaredd	Llanilltud
Llandeilo	Llanfeugan	Llanina
Llandinier	Llanfrothen	Llanismel
Llandridian	Llanfyrnach	Llanllawddog
Llandrillo	Llanfyllin	Llanllechid
Llandrinio	Llangadfan	Llanlleonfel
Llandybie	Llangadog	Llanllugan
Llandyfalle	Llanganten	Llanllwchaiarn
Llandyfân	Llangathen	Llanllwni
Llandyfeisant	Llangattock	Llan-llŷr
Llandyfriog	Llangeitho	Llanidan
Llandygwydd	Llangeler	Llan-non
Llandysilio(gogo)	Llangelynnin	Llanrug
Llandysul	Llangenau	Llanrhystud
Llanddarog	Llangennech	Llansadwrn
Llanddeged	Llanglydwen	Llansawel

Llansteffan	Llanedi	Llangyndeyrn
Llantysilio	Llanegryn	Llangynfelyn
Llanwenog	Llanegwad	Llanwrin
Llanwinio	Llaneleu	Llanwrtyd
Llanwnnog	Llangunnor	Llanwrthwl
Llanwrda	Llangurig	Llanwyddelan
Llanddeti	Llangwril	Llanwyddyn
Llanddingad	Llangybi	Llanychhaearn

Llanaber :	church of the stream's mouth
Llan Bach Howey :	church of river bend of r. Hywi
Llanbadarn Fynydd :	St. Padarn's church of the mountain
Llanbadarn Garreg :	St. Padarn's church of the rock
Llanbadarn Trefeglwys:	St. Padarn's church; home of church
Llanbadarn y Creuddyn:	St. Padarn's church; creuddyn— pigs' fold
Llanbedr Castell-paen:	St. Peter's church; castle of Payne
Llanbedr Pont Steffan:	St. Peter's church of Stephen's bridge
Llanbedr Ystrad Yw:	St. Peter's church in vale of yews
Llan-bedw:	church; birches (or Bedw—r. name)
Llanbryn-mair:	llan—church; bryn—hill; Mair—Mary
Llan-crwys:	church of the cross
Llandefaelog Tre'r-graig:	St. Maelog's church; home of rock
Llandeilo Abercywyn:	St. Teilo's church at mouth of r. Cywyn
Llandeilo Graban:	St. Teilo's church; graban—corn marigold
Llandeilo'r-fân:	St. Teilo's church on r. Bawan
Llandinam (Llandinan):	church of small fort enclosure
Llandovery (Llanymddyfri):	church among the waters
Llan-dre (Llodre):	church in bottom land
Llandrindod: '	church of the Trinity
Llanddeusant:	church of two saints
Llanddewi Abergwesyn:	St. David's church; mouth of r. Gwesyn (Shepherd)
Llanddewibrefi:	St. David's church on the r. Brefi
Llanddewi'r-cwm:	St. David's church in the valley
Llanddewi Ystradenni:	St David's church; vale of Nynnid
Llanddowror:	church of the waters
Llanddulas:	church on r. Dulas
Llanddwywe-is-y-graig:	church of St. Dwywe below the rock
Llanfair-ar-y-bryn:	St. Mary's church on the hill
Llanfair Caereinion:	St. Mary's church; fort of Einion
Llanfair Clydogau';	St. Mary's church; clywedogau— noisy streams
Llanfair Nant-gwyn:	St. Mary's church of white stream
Llanfair Nant-y-gof:	St. Mary's church of smith's brook
Llanfair Orllwyn:	St. Mary's church; orllwyn—big wood
Llanfair Pwllgwyngyll :	St. Mary's church; pool of the white hazel trees

Llan-faes:	church in meadow
Llanfarian:	church of beach or moraine
Llanfechain:	church in plain of r. Cain
Llanfechan:	church; small
Llanfihangel Abergwesyn:	St. Michael's church; mouth of r. Gwesyn
Llanfihangel Aberbythych:	St. Michael's church; mouth of r. Bythych
Llanfihangel-ar-arth (Iorath):	St. Michael's church; Iorath—pers. name
Llanfihangel Bryn Pabuan:	St. Michael's church; hill of Pabuan
Llanfihangel Cwm-du:	St.-Michael's church; dark valley
Llanfihangel Dyffryn Arwy:	St. Michael's church in Arwy valley
Llanfihangel Helygen:	St. Michael's church; helygen—willows; pers. name
Llanfihangel Nant Brân:	St. Michael's church on r. Brân
Llanfihangel Rhos-y-corn:	St. Michael's church; moor of the peak
Llanfihangel Rhyd Ithon:	St. Michael's church ford of r. Ithon
Llanfihangel Tal-y-llyn:	St. Michael's church; head of lake
Llanfihangel-uwch-Gwili:	St. Michael's church above r. Gwili
Llanfihangel y Creuddyn:	St. Michael's church; hill of pigsty
Llanfihangel-y-Pennant:	St. Michael's church head of valley
Llanfihangel-y-traethau:	St. Michael's church of the beaches
Llanfihangel yng Ngwynfa:	St. Michael's church in fair plain
Llanfihangel Ystrad:	St. Michael's church in the vale
Llanfilo:	church of Milo (pers. name)
Llanfor:	big church
Llanfynydd:	church of the mountain
Llangamarch:	church of r. Camarch (march—horse)
Llangasty Tal-y-llyn:	church of St. Gasteyn; end of lake
Llangoed:	church of wood
Llangoedmor:	church of big wood
Llangollen:	church of St. Collen (hazel tree)
Llangors:	church of the swamp
Llangorwen:	(uncertain) see 'Corwen'?
Llangower:	church of St. Cywair
Llangwm:	valley of the church
Llangwnadl (Nant Gwyn Hoedl) :	nant (valley); Gwyn Hoedl (pers. name)
Llangwyryfon:	church of the virgins
Llanhamlach (prob. Llanamlwch):	church of swamp
Llanllugan:	church of Llugan (light)
Llan-llwch:	church of swamp or lake
Llannerch:	a glade or clearing
Llannerch Brochwel:	glade of Brochwel (pers. name)
Llannerch Celli:	glade in hazel trees
Llannerch-fraith:	mottled glade

Llannerch Hudol:	enchanted glade
Llannerch-lwyd:	holy or grey glade
Llannerch-wen:	fair glade
Llannerch-y-cawr:	giant's glade
Llannerch-y-medd :	glade of the mead (drink)
Llanpumpsaint:	church of five saints
Llan-saint :	llan—church; saint—saints
Llansanffraid Deuddwr:	St. Bridget's church of two rivers
Llansanffraid-ym-Mechain:	St. Bridget's church in land of r. Cain
Llansbyddyd:	prob. church of the hawthorn tree
Llanshiver (Llan Llys Ifor):	church of Ifor's court
Llan Shon Dorthy:	Shon Dorddu (pers. name)
Llanthony (Llan Nant Hodni):	church of r. Hodni
Llanuwchllyn:	church above lake
Llan-wern:	church of the marsh or alders
Llanybydder:	(uncertain) byddar—deaf ones
Llan-y-cil:	church of the recess
Llanyfelin:	church of the mill
Llanymynech:	church of the monks
Llanynis:	church of the river meadow
Llanystumdwy :	llan - church; ystum - bend; Dwy - name of river (goddess)
Llanyre:	poss. church of Llŷr or 'hir'—long
llawr:	low ground in valley
Llawr Betws:	low ground:bead house
Llawr-y-cwm:	valley bottom
Llawr-y-glyn:	bottom of glen
llech:	a flat stone
Llech-faen:	flat stone
Llech-gron:	round stone
Llechog:	rocky place
Llechryd:	stone ford or brook
Llechwedd:	a hillside
Llechwedd-crin:	dry hillside
Lleyn :	land of the Lageni (tribe)
Llowes (Llywes):	name of a saint
Lloyney (Llwyni):	bushes
Lluest:	small hill farm; a hut
Lluestbeili:	enclosure of hill cabin
Lluest Dôl Gwiail:	cabin of meadow of canes
Lluestdduallt:	cabin of black slope
Lluestnewydd:	new cabin or hill farm
Lluest Tŷ-mawr:	hill farm of big house
Lluest-wen:	fair hill farm
Lluest Uchaf:	higher hill farm

Lluestcerrig:	hill farm of the stones
Lluest-y-graig:	hill farm of the rock
Llundain-fach:	little London
Llwybr Heulwen:	sunny path
Llwydcoed:	grey wood
Llwydiarth:	grey headland
Llwyn:	a bush or grove
Llwyncelyn:	holly bush
Llwynceubren:	grove of hollow trunk
Llwyn-coch:	red grove
Llwyncwta:	short wood
Llwyncyntefin:	grove of earliest times
Llwyndafydd:	grove of Dafydd
Llwyn-derw:	oak grove
Llwyndyrys:	intricate or tangled grove
Llwynfedwen:	birch grove
Llwyn Garth-fawr:	grove of big headland
Llwyn-glas:	green grove
Llwyn-gwyn:	white grove
Llwyn Iago:	grove of Iago (James)
Llwyn Neuadd:	grove of hall
Llwyn-onn:	ash grove
Llwyn Pentre:	village grove
Llwynrhydowen:	grove of Owen's ford
Llwyn-tew:	thick grove
Llwyn-y-brain:	grove of the crows
Llwyn-y-gôg:	grove of cuckoo
Llwyn-y-groes:	grove of cross
Llwyn yr Ehedydd:	grove of the lark
Llwyn-yr-hwrdd:	grove of the ram
Llyfnant:	smooth stream
Llygad Cleddy:	source of r. Cleddau
Llymwynt (Llin-went):	flax meadow
Llyn: a lake or pool	

Aran: hill ridge	Login: impure water
Berwyn: snow top	Mawr: large
Carw: stag	Newydd: new
Cnwch: mound	Pen-maen: rock end
Conglog: corners	Pryfed: insects
Cwmbychan: small glen	Rhuddnant: red brook
Cwm Llwch: valley lake	Tegid: (pers. name)
Diffwys: precipice	Teifi: (river name)
Du: black	Tywarchen : turf
Dwfn: deep	Vyrnwy: (river name)
Eiddew. (pers. name)	y Bugail: the shepherd
Eiddwen: (pers. name)	y Fign: the marsh
Fanod: (pers. name)	y Gorlan: the fold
Ffridd: hill pasture	y Gwaith: the mine
Gafr: goat	y Morynion: the maids
Gorast: waste land	y Mynydd: the mountain

Gwyddon: (pers. name)	yr Oerfel: the cold
Gwyn: white	y Tarw: the bull
Heilyn (pers. name)	y Waun: the moor

-Brianne:	poss. of the mountains
- Coch Hwyad :	of the grouse . . .
- Craig y Pistyll :	of rock of spring
- Cwm Mynach :	of monk's valley
- Llygad Rheidol :	of r. Rheidol source
- Nant Ddeiliog :	of leafy valley
- y Cerrig Llwydion :	of the grey rocks
- y Clogwyn Brith :	of mottled crag
- y Fan Fach :	of the small peak
- y Fan Fawr :	of the big peak
- y Garnedd Uchaf :	of highest cairn
- y Tri Greyenyn :	of three pebbles
Llynclys :	from "llwnc" (to swallow)
llys :	court or mansion
Llys Arthur :	Arthur's court
Llysdinam (-dinan):	fortified court
Llys-teg :	fair court
Llystin :	small court
Llys Ucha :	upper court
Llys-wen :	white court
Llywel :	name of a saint
Llywernog :	place of foxes
Machynlleth :	the plain of Cynllaith (pers. name)
Maelienydd :	land of Maelien (pers. name)
Maen :	a rock
Maen Beuno :	rock of Beuno (pers. name)
Maenclochog :	rock; clochog—as of a bell
Maen-du :	black stone
Maenhinon :	rock of r. Hinon
Maen-llwyd :	grey rock
Maenol :	ancient division of land
Maenordeilo :	maenor—an ancient land division; deilo—Teilo (pers. name)
Maen-serth :	rock; serth—steep
Maentwrog :	rock of Twrog(pers. name)
Maerdy :	house of mayor or steward
Maes :	a field (orig. unenclosed)
Maesbrynar :	fallow field
Maes-carn :	field of the cairn
Maes Celynnen :	field of holly tree
Maesderwen :	oak meadow
Maes-glas :	green meadow
Maes-gwyn :	white meadow

Maes Machreth :	meadow of Machreth (pers. name)
Maes-mawr :	big meadow
Maesmelan :	prob. meadow of Melan (pers. name)
Maesmynis :	prob. meadow of Mynis (pers. name)
Maes-nant :	meadow of the stream
Maes-poeth :	warm meadow (burnt)
Maes-teg :	fair meadow
Maestregymer :	meadow of homestead at r. confluence
Maesyberllan :	meadow of the orchard
Maes y Carneddau :	meadow of the cairns
Maesydd (Meusydd):	meadows
Maesycrugiau :	meadow of the cairns
Maesyfed (Radnor) :	maes—meadow; hyfaidd—bold (pers. name)
Maesyfelin :	meadow of the mill
Maes-y-groes :	meadow of the cross or crossroad
Maes y Neuadd :	meadow of the hall
Maesypandy :	meadow of the fulling-mill
Maesyperthi :	meadow of the hedges or bushes
Maes yr Awel :	meadow of the breeze
Maes yr Helm :	meadow of the rick
Maesyronnen :	meadow of the ash-tree
Malltraeth :	sandy or poor land
Mallwyd :	grey plain or field
Manafon :	ma—a plain; Nafon (pers. name)
Man-teg :	fair place
Marchnant :	Name of a river (march—horse)
Mardu (Maerdy) :	steward's house
Mathafarn :	field of tavern
Mathrafal :	triangular field or plain
mawn :	peat
Mawnog :	place of peat
Mechain :	plain of river Cain
Meidrim :	middle ridge
Meifod :	middle or half-way dwelling
Meirionnydd :	the land of Meirion, a Welsh prince
Meity :	half-way house; a lodging
Melin :	a mill
Melindwr :	water-mill
Melin-y-ddôl :	mill of the meadow
Melin-y-gloch :	mill of river Cloch (babbling)
Melin-y-grug :	mill of the heather
Melin y-wig :	mill of the wood; or mill of bay
Menai :	poss. flowing water
Merthyr :	a martyr; a martyr's grave
Merthyr Cynog :	burial place of St. Cynog
Milltir Gerrig :	mile—rocks

Minffordd :	edge of road
Min Ffrwd :	stream edge
Min Gwern :	edge of marsh
Min-y-don :	edge of the wave or sea
Min-y-llyn :	edge of the lake
Mochdre :	homestead of pigs
Moel :	bare hilltop or hill
Moel Blaen Tafolog :	bare hill at source of river Tafolog (dock-leaves)
Moel Dinmael :	bare hill of chief's fort
Moel Ddôl-wen :	bare hill of the white meadow
Moel Eiddew :	bare hill of Eiddew (pers. name)
Moel Feliarth :	bare hill of sweet or honey headland
Moelfre :	bare hill
Moel Frochan :	bare hill of wild stream
Moel Fronllwyd :	bare hill-top with brown hillside
Moelfryn :	bare topped hill
Moel Geufron :	enclosed hillside of bare mountain
Moel Gwigoedd :	woods of the bare topped hill
Moel Hebog :	bare hill of the hawk
Moel Iart (garth) :	headland of bare hill
Moel Llyfnant :	bare hill of river Llyfnant (smooth-flowing)
Moel Main :	bare hill of the rock
Moel Sych :	dry, bare hill
Moel-y-bryn :	bare top of the hill
Moel y Cerrig Duon :	bare hill of the black stones
Moelydd :	bare hilltops
Moelydd Blaen Tafolog :	bare tops of source of r. Tafolog
Moel y Garth :	bare hill of the enclosure or headland
Moel y Gest :	bare hill of the hollow
Moel-y-god :	lowland of the bare hill
Moel y Golfa :	bare hill; branches or boughs
Moel y Llyn :	bare hill of the lake
Moel y Sant :	bare hill of the saint
Monachdy (Mynachdy):	monastery
Morlan :	seashore
Morfa Bychan :	little bog or sea-marsh
Morfa Nefyn :	sea marsh of Nefyn (pers. name)
Mostyn :	marsh of the homestead
Mwnt :	mound or hill
Myddfai :	meadow of the round hollow
mynydd :	a mountain
Mynydd Brith :	mottled mountain
Mynydd Bychan :	little mountain
Mynydd Cerrig Llwydion :	mountain of grey stones
Mynydd Cil-cwm :	mountain of valley recess or r. source
Mynydd Clogau :	mountain of the crags

Mynydd Clywedog :	mountain of river Clywedog (noisy)
Mynydd Coch :	red mountain
Mynydd Dyfnant :	mountain of river Dyfnant (deep valley)
Mynydd Eithaf :	furthest mountain
Mynydd Esgair :	mountain of the ridge
Mynydd Esgeiriau :	mountain of the ridges
Mynydd Garth Pwt:	mountain of small headland
Mynydd Hir :	long mountain
Mynydd Lluest-fach :	mountain of the little cabin
Mynydd Llyn Coch Hwyad :	mynydd—mountain; llyn— lake; coch hwyad—grouse
Mynydd Llwytgoed :	mountain of the grey wood
Mynydd Llys :	mountain of mansion (or llus—bilberries)
Mynydd Mawr :	big mountain
Mynydd Penpistyll :	mountain of head of the spring
Mynydd Rhiw Saeson :	mountain of the ascent of the English
Mynydd Talyglannau:	mountain of the front or end of r. banks.
Mynydd Tri Arglwydd:	mountain of the three lords
Mynydd Troed :	mountain; foot
Mynydd Ty'r Sais :	mountain of the house of the Englishman
Mynydd Waun-fawr :	mountain of the big moorland or meadow
Mynydd y Cemais :	mountain of the river bend
Mynydd y Defaid :	mountain of the sheep
Mynydd y Gadfa :	mountain where flock is driven
Mynydd y Glyn :	mountain of the glen
Mynydd yr Eithin :	mountain of the gorse
Mynydd yr Hendre :	mountain of the main or winter home
Mynydd yr Heol :	mountain of the road
Nancall :	valley of river Call
Nanmor :	big valley
Nantcol (nant-coel):	stream or valley of Coel (pers. name)
Nannerth :	bears' stream
Nanneu :	streams; valleys
Nant:	a stream; small valley containing stream
Nant y Barcut:	stream of the kite
Nant Brithyll:	stream of the trout
Nant Brochen :	stream name (wild and foamy)
Nant Caletwr:	name of stream (rough water)
Nant Carfan :	name of stream (border ridge)
Nant Cerrig-y-Gro:	stream of pebbles or gravel
Nant Cerrig-y-groes:	stream of rocks of the cross
Nant Cerrig-y-frân :	stream of the rocks of the crow
Nant Cwm-du:	stream of the black valley

Nant-ddu :	black valley or stream
Nanteos :	valley of the nightingale
Nant Ffrancon :	valley or stream of the soldier
Nant Ffridd-y-Castell:	stream of the pasture of the castle
Nantgaredig :	nant—stream; caredig—kind
Nant Gerwin :	a wild stream
Nant-glas :	green valley
Nant-gwyn :	white stream
Nant Hesgog :	stream of sedges
Nant-hir:	long stream
Nant-llech :	rocky stream
Nant-mawr :	big stream
Nant y Meirch :	stream of the horses
Nantmel:	prob. stream of mael (a chieftain)
Nant Nadroedd :	stream of snakes
Nantperfedd:	stream of middle land
Nant Rhaeadr:	stream of waterfall
Nant Rhyd Rhos-lan:	valley of the moor stream
Nant Saeson :	stream of the English
Nant Tawelan :	river name (quiet)
Nant Troedyresgair :	stream of the foot of the ridge
Nant y Bachws :	stream of the nook or bend
Nantybeddau :	stream of the graves
Nantycriba :	stream of the crests
Nantycytiau :	stream of the huts
Nant y Dryslwyn :	stream of the tanglewood
Nant y Dugoed:	stream of the black wood
Nant y Filltir :	brook a mile long
Nant y Fyda :	stream of the wild bee
Nant-y-ffin :	stream of the border
Nant y Gader :	stream of the fort
Nant y Geifr :	stream of the goats
Nant y Llyn :	stream of the lake
Nant y Moch :	stream of the pigs
Nant y Mynach :	stream of the monk
Nant yr Afallen :	stream of the apple-tree
Nant yr Eira :	stream of the snow
Nant yr Haidd :	stream of the barley
Nant yr hendy :	stream of the old house
Nantyrhafod :	stream of the summer-house
Nantyronnen :	stream of the ash-tree
Nantystalwyn :	stream of the stallion
Nefyn :	a personal name
Neint :	stream
Neuadd :	a hall or mansion
Neuadd Glan Gwy :	hall of the bank of river Wye
Neuadd-goch :	red hall
Neuadd-lwyd :	grey hall

Neuadd-wen :	white hall
Nythfa :	nesting place
Ochr-cefn :	ridge side
Ochr-lwyd :	grey hillside
Oerffrwd :	cold stream
Ogof Llanymynech :	cave of church of the monks
Pandy :	fulling-mill
Pandy Tudur :	fulling mill of Tudur
Pannau :	hollows
Pant :	a hollow or valley
Pantcrugnant :	hollow of the cairn stream
Pant-glas :	green hollow
Pang-gwyn :	white hollow
Pantiau :	hollows
Pantle :	place of hollow
Pant-mawr :	big hollow
Pantperthog :	hollow of hedges or bushes
Pant-poeth :	warm or burnt hollow
Pantrhiw-goch :	hollow of the red hillside
Panty :	house of hollow
Pantybeiliau :	hollow of the enclosures
Pantybriallu :	hollow of the primroses
Pant y Bwch :	hollow of the buck
Pantycelyn :	hollow of the holly-trees
Pant-y-crai :	hollow of the fresh water
Pant-y-dwr :	hollow of the water
Pant-y-Fedw :	hollow of the birch trees
Pant-y-ffridd :	hollow of the mountain pasture
Pantyffynnon :	hollow of the well
Pantygesail :	hollow of the mountain recess
Pantyneuadd :	hollow of the hall
Pant yr Athro :	hollow of the teacher
Pantyrhendre :	hollow of the main or winter home
Pant-yr-ynn :	hollow of the ash-trees
Pantysgallog :	hollow of the thistles
Pant-y-waun :	hollow of the meadow
Pant-y-wern :	hollow of the bog
Parc :	a park
Parc-gwyn :	white parkland
Parciau bach :	little parklands
Parc Newydd :	new parkland
Parc-y-drain :	parkland of the thorns
Parc-y-maen :	parkland of the rock
Parc-y-rhiw :	parkland of the hillside
Partrisio :	prob. church of Isio or Ossui
Pedair-ffordd :	four roads

Pegwn Mawr :	big peak
Pembrey (Pen-bre)	top of the hill
Penally (Pen Alun):	pen—head; Alun (pers. name)
Penarlâg (Hawarden) :	the hilltop of Alaog (pers. name)
Pen-arth :	head of the enclosure or promontory
Pen Bwlch y Groes :	head of the pass of the cross
Pencader :	head of seat or fort
Pen-cae :	head of the field
Pen Cae Coety :	pen—head; cae—field; coety—house in wood
Pen Cae-du :	head of the black field
Pencarreg :	head of the rock
Pencastell :	castle end
Pencelli :	head of grove (hazel)
Pencerrig y Ffynnon :	head of the rocks of the well
Pencloddiau :	head of the mountain banks
Pen-coed :	head of the wood
Pen-cnwc :	top of the knoll
Pen-craig :	head of the rock
Pen Cwm yr Hafod :	head of the valley of the summer house
Penderyn :	(uncertain): bird's end; end of two headlands
Pendine (Pentywyn) :	end of sand dunes
Pen-dre :	end of top of town or homestead
Penegoes (Pen-y-goes) :	head of the mountain spur
Penffordd-wen :	head of the road (wen-fair)
Pengenffordd :	head of ridge road
Pen-gwern :	head of the marsh or alders
Penhelig :	head of the willow trees
Peniarth :	head of the enclosure or headland
Penisacyffin :	lower end of boundary
Penisa'r-cwm :	lower end of valley
Penisa'rpentre :	lower end of the village
Penisa'r-plwyf :	lower end of parish
Pen-lan :	top of hill
Penllannerch :	head of the glade
Penllidiardiau :	head of the gates
Pen Lluest y Carn :	head of the cabin of the cairn
Pen-llwyn :	head of the grove
Penmachno (Pen-nant Machno) :	Pennant - head of valley; Machno (pers. name)
Pen-maen :	head of rock
Pen Maen-wern :	head of the rock of the marsh
Penmaen-mawr :	head of the big rock
Penmorfa :	head of the sea-shore
Pennal :	region of the enemy
Pennant :	head of the stream or valley

Pen Nant Melangell:	head of Melangell stream (pers. name)
Pen Nant-twrch:	head of Twrch stream or valley (burrowing)
Penoyre (Pen-aur):	golden headland
Penparcau :	head of the park lands
Penpentre:	top of village
Pen-pont :	end of bridge
Penrallt :	top of the slope
Penrhiw Bwllfa :	top or end of hillside of pit or pool place
Penrhiwcarnau :	top of the hillside of the cairns
Pen-rhos :	head of the moorland
Penrhos-goch :	head of the red moorland
Penrhyd :	river end; ford end
Penrhyn-coch :	red promontory
Penrhyndeudraeth :	promontory of the two beaches
Pen-sarn :	head of the paved way
Pentre :	a village
Pentre-bach :	little village
Pentre Caeau :	village of fields
Pentre Celyn :	village of river Celyn (holly trees or p. name)
Pentre Cribarth :	village of mountain crest
Pentre-cwrt :	village of the court
Pentre Cyffin :	village of the border
Pentrefoelas :	village of the green, bare summit
Pentre Gwenlais :	village of river Gwenlais (fair water)
Pentre Hirin :	village of river Hirin (long)
Pentre-hwnt :	yonder village
Pentrehyling (Heilyn):	village of Heilyn (pers. name)
Pentre Iago :	village of Iago (James)
Pentre Isaf :	lower village
Pentre Lludw :	village of ashes
Pentre-nant :	village of the stream
Pentre'r-beirdd :	village of the poets
Pentre'rfelin :	village of the mill
Pentre'r-gof :	village of the smith
Pentre Tŷ-gwyn :	village of the white house
Pentre-wern :	village of the marsh or alders
Pen-twyn :	end of top of hill
Pen-y-banc :	top of the bank
Pen-y-bont :	bridge end
Pen-y-bryn :	top of the hill
Pen-y-cae :	end of the field
Pen y Garreg :	head of the rock
Pen-y-garth :	head of the headland or enclosure
Pen-y-groes :	head of the crossroads
Penygwryd :	pen-head; gwryd-length of outstretched arms

Peraidd Fynydd :	sweet mountain
Persondy :	vicarage
Perthi :	hedges or bushes
Perth-y-bi :	hedge of the magpies
Pigyns :	peaks
Pistyll :	well or spring
Pistyll-du :	black spring
Pistyll Graig-ddu :	spring of the black rock
Pistyll-gwyn :	white spring
Pistyll Rhaeadr :	spring of the waterfall
Plas :	a mansion
Plas-bach :	little mansion
Plas-coch :	red mansion
Plasdinan :	mansion of little fort
Plas Dolanog :	mansion of winding stream
Plas Dolguog :	mansion of meadow or r. Guog, (beloved)
Plas-du :	black hall
Plas Esgair :	mansion of the ridge
Plas-gwyn :	white or fair mansion
Plas Hyfryd :	pleasant mansion
Plas Iolyn :	mansion of Iolyn (pers. name)
Plas Llwynowen :	mansion of Owen's grove
Plas Machynlleth :	ma - plain; Cynllaith - pers. name
Plasnewydd :	new mansion
Plas Rhiw Saeson :	mansion of hill of the Englaish
Plas-y-bryn :	mansion of the hill
Plas y Dinas :	mansion of the fort
Plas yng Nghaeau :	mansion in the fields
Plwmp :	a pump
Plynlumon(Pumlumon):	five peaks
pont :	a bridge
Pontardulais :	bridge over the river Dulais (black water)
Pont ar Elan :	bridge over river Elan (goddess's name)
Pontarfynach :	bridge over river Mynach (a monk)
Pontargothi :	bridge over river Cothi (issuing out)
Pont ar Ithon :	bridge over river Ithon (name of a god)
Pontarllechau :	bridge over r. Llechau (rocky stream)
Pont Cynon :	bridge over river Cynon (pers. name)
Pont Dôl-goch :	bridge of the red meadow
Ponterwyd :	bridge of 'Orwid', an old fem. personal name
Pont-faen :	stone bridge
Pontgarreg :	stone bridge (or bridge of the stone)
Pont Glan Tanat :	bridge of Tanat bank
Pont Llogel :	bridge of the house-wall
Pontmaen-du :	bridge of the black rock
Pont Moelfre :	bridge of the bare mountain
Pontneathvaughan (Pontneddfechan):	bridge of lesser river Nedd

Pontnewydd :	new bridge
Pont Pandy Llwydiarth :	bridge of fulling-mill of grey headland
Pontrobert :	bridge of Robert
Pontrhydfendigaid :	bridge of the blessed ones
Pont Rhyd-y-groes :	bridge of the ford of the cross
Pontsenni :	bridge of Senni river (prob. p. name)
Pont Siân :	bridge of Siân (pers. name)
Pontsticill :	bridge of stile
Pont-twrch :	bridge of river Twrch (burrowing)
Pont Tyweli :	bridge of river Tyweli (bold stream)
Pontwillim :	bridge of William (pers. name)
Pontyates:	bridge of Yates (pers. name)
Pont y Pentre :	bridge of the village
Pontyrogof :	bridge of the cave
Pont-y-wal :	(uncert.) bridge of the wall
Porth :	a gateway or harbour
Porthmadog :	the harbour of Maddocks
Porth-mawr :	big gateway
Porth-y-rhyd :	gateway of the ford
Powys :	a tribal name; pau - a country
Pren-gwyn :	white or fair tree
Prestatyn :	(non-Welsh) priest's town
Prysgduon :	black brushwood
Prysgol :	place of brushwood
Prysor :	heap of brushwood
Pumsaint :	five saints
Pwll :	a pit or pool
Pwllan :	a small pool
Pwll-glas :	green or blue pool
Pwll-gloew :	shining pool
Pwllheli :	salt-water pool
Pwll Iwrch :	pool or river Iwrch (roe-buck)
Pwll Llaca :	muddy pool
Pwll Melyn :	yellow or brown pool
Pwll-trap :	pool or pit of step (rise in Ground)
Pwll-y-bryn :	pool of the hill
Pwll-y-calch :	lime-pit
Pyllan :	little pool
Pyllan-clais :	pool of cleft or ditch
Pyllan-mawn :	pool or pit of peat
Pysgodlyn :	fish pool
Pytin :	(from Norman name; du-black; glas - green; gwyn - white)
Rhandir-mwyn :	land of minerals
Rhayader (Rhaeadr):	a waterfall
Rheol (Yr heol) :	the road

Rhewl (yr heol) :	the street or road
Rhigos :	place of heather
Rhiw :	a hillside
Rhiw Defeity :	hillside of sheep pasture
Rhiw-fawr :	big hillside
Rhiwfelen :	brown or yellow hillside
Rhiw-garn :	hillside of the cairn
Rhiwgriafol :	hillside of mountain ash-trees
Rhiwhiraeth :	hillside of river Hiraeth
Rhiwiau :	hillsides
Rhiw-las :	green hillside
Rhiw-pant :	hillside of hollow
Rhiw Saeth :	hillside of river Saeth
Rhiw-wen :	fair hillside
Ro, y :	place of pebbles
Rhobell :	narrow ridge like a saddle
Rhos :	moorland
Rhos-ddu :	black moorland
Rhos-fawr :	big moorland
Rhos-goch :	red moorland
Rhos-hir :	long moorland
Rhosllannerchrugog :	moorland of the heather-glade
Rhos-maen :	moorland of the rock
Rhosmeheryn :	moorland of river Myherin (prob. pers. name)
Rhos Pen Bwa :	moorland of head of arch (Bwa=pers. name)?
Rhostryfan :	moorland of the rounded peak
Rhos Saith Maen :	moorland of the seven stones
Rhostyno :	flat moorland
Rhos y Brithdir :	moorland of the mottled land
Rhosygarreg :	moorland of the rock
Rhosgelynnen :	moorland of the holly-tree
Rhos-y-bol :	moorland of the cavity
Rhosygwaliau :	moorland of the walls
Rhos y Gweision :	moorland of the servants
Rhos y Pentref :	moorland of the village
rhyd :	a ford or stream
Rhydargaeau :	stream near the fields
Rhyd Cefn-du :	stream of the black hillside
Rhydcymerau :	ford of the confluences
Rhyd-ddu:	black ford
Rhydescin (hescyn):	stream of peat-bog
Rhydfelin :	mill of the ford or stream
Rhyd-hir :	long stream or ford
Rhydlewis :	ford of Lewis (pers. name)
Rhydlydan :	wide ford
Rhyd Moel-ddu :	stream of the black bare hill

Rhydodyn :	ford or stream of the lime-kiln
Rhydoldog :	winding stream
Rhydolffordd :	ford : meadow : road
Rhydspence :	prob. ford of Spence (pers. name)
Rhydyberry (Rhydybere) :	stream of the kite
Rhyd-y-cil :	stream of the recess
Rhydyclafdy :	ford or stream of the hospital
Rhyd-y-cwm :	stream of the valley
Rhyd-y-fro :	stream or ford of the vale
Rhyd-y-groes :	stream of the cross or crossroads
Rhyd y Llechau :	ford of the flat stones
Rhyd-y-maen :	ford of the stone
Rhyd y Meirch :	ford of the horses
Rhyd-y-mwyn :	ford or stream of the mineral ore
Rhydypennau :	**ford of the heads (heads of cattle)**
Rhydyronnen :	ford of the ash-tree
Rhydywernen :	ford of the marsh (or alder)
Rhysnant (Rhosnant):	stream of moorland
Rhuallt :	poss. red hill
Rhuddlan :	red bank
Rhyl :	prob. the hill
Ruabon (Rhiwabon) :	the ascent of Abon (pers. name)
Rug, y :	place of heather
Saith Maen :	seven stones
San-clêr :	St. Clear's
Sarn :	a paved way
Sarnau :	paved ways
Scwd yr Eira :	snow waterfall
Sgethrog :	rough, rocky (or from pers. name)
Sgwylfa (Disgwylfa):	watching place
Slwch :	(prob. is-lwch — below lake)
Struet:	(unknown — written 'ystrywiaid' in 15th cent.)
Swydd :	a district
Swyddffynnon :	district of the well
Sycharth :	dry headland or enclosure
Sychcwm :	dry valley
Sychnant :	stream that dries up
Sychtyn :	sych—dry; tyn—small farm
Tafolog :	place of dock-leaves
Tafol-wern :	marsh of dock-leaves
Tai-bach :	little houses
Taihirion :	long houses
Tai'r Bull :	houses of the Bull (public house)
Tair Carreg :	three stones
Tairderwen :	three oak trees (or houses of the oak)

Tair Ffynnon :	three wells or houses of the well
Tai-rhos :	houses of moorland
(tâl):	end : front : brow
Talardd :	enclosure at brow of hill
Tal-cefn :	brow of hillside
Talcen Llwydiarth :	brown enclosure at brow of hill
Tal-coed :	woods at brow of hill
Talerddig :	small enclosure at brow of hill
Talgarth :	enclosure at brow of hill
Talgarreg :	rock at brow of hill
Talley (Talyllychau) :	waters (lakes) at foot of hill
Tal-sarn :	causeway (paved road) at brow of hill
Talsarnau :	causeways at brow of hill
Talwen :	fair brow of hill
Talwrn :	rocky place, cock-fighting pit at brow of hill
Tal-y-bont :	bridge at brow of hill
Tal-y-llyn :	lake below brow of hill
Talyrnau :	rocky places at brow of hill
Tal-y-wern :	marshland below brow of hill
Tandderwen :	below the oak
Tanglwys :	a personal name
Tan-lan :	below the slope
Tan Troed :	below the Troed mountain (troed-foot)
Tan-y-bwlch :	below the pass
Tanycaeau :	below the fields
Tan-y-cefn :	below the ridge
Tan-y-clawdd :	below the mountainside or ditch
Tan-y-fron :	below the hillside
Tan-y-ffordd :	below the road
Tan-y-ffridd :	below the mountain pasture
Tan-y-graig :	under the rock or cliff
Tanygrisiau :	below the steps
Tan-y-groes :	below the crossroad
Tan-y-llan :	below the church or village
Tan-yr-allt :	below the hillside or wood
Tap y Gigfran :	ledge of the raven
Tarren :	a rocky hillside : a cliff
Tarren Bwlch-gwyn :	rock of the white pass
Tawelfan :	quiet place
Teirtref :	three homesteads
Tenby (Dinbych) :	small fort
tir :	land
Tirabad :	land of the abbot
Tircelyn :	land of holly trees
Tirnewydd :	new land
Tir Rhiwiog :	hilly land

Tirymynach :	land of the monk
tomen :	a mound
Tomen Ugre :	mound of Ugre (pers. name)
Torbant :	break of the hollow
Torpantau :	tor—a break; bant (pant)—hollow
Towyn :	place of sand; beach
Traean-glas :	a third part; green
Traean-mawr :	a third part; big
Trallwm (or Trallong) :	a marsh
Trannon :	a river name (strong-flowing)
Trap :	a step; rise in ground
Trawscoed :	cross wood
Trawsfynydd :	in direction of or across mountain
Trawsgelli :	in direction of the copse
Trawsnant :	across stream or valley
tre :	a homestead; a home; a town
Tre-allt :	homestead of the hillside or wood
Trearddur :	homestead of Iarddur (pers. name)
Treberfydd :	homestead in middle-land
Tre-coed :	home of the wood
Trederwen :	home of the oak-tree
Trederwen Feibion :	home of the oak of the sons
Tredomen :	homestead of mound
Trefach :	small homestead
Trefecca :	home of Becca (pers. name)
Trefechan :	little homestead
Trefeglwys :	home of the church
Trefeinion :	homestead of Einon (pers. name)
Trefenter :	tre-home; fenter-venture
Treflyn :	lake of homestead
Trefnant :	stream of homestead
Tre-foel :	homestead of bare hill
Tre-ffin :	homestead of the border
Trefonnen :	home of the ash tree
Trefor :	big homestead
Trefriw :	homestead of hillside
Tre-gaer :	homestead of the fort
Tregaron :	town or home of Caron (pers. name)
Tre-goed :	homestead of the wood
Tregrugyn :	homestead of small cairn
Tre-gwynt :	windy homestead
Tregynon :	home of Cynon (pers. name)
Tre-haidd :	homestead of barley
Trehelig :	home of willow trees
Trehelig-gro :	willow home of gravel or pebbles
Trelawnyd (Newmarket) :	home of Lawnyd (pers. name)
Trelystan :	home of Elystan (pers. name)
Tremadoc :	town of Maddocks

Tre-maen :	stone homestead
Trefnannau :	homestead of the streams
Trenewydd :	new town or homestead
Tre'r-ddôl :	homestead of the meadow
Tre-saith :	homestead of river Saith
Tre Taliesin :	homestead of Taliesin (pers. name)
Treuddyn :	a dwelling place
Trevaughan (Tre	tre - home; Fychan (pers. name
Fychan :	- small)
Trevayne (Tre-faen):	stone homestead
Tre-wern :	homestead of marsh or alders
Trewylan :	home of Gwylan (pers. name)
Trewythan :	home of Gwythan (pers. name)
Troedrhiwdalar :	foot of the slope of the headland
Troedrhiw-las :	foot of the green slope
Troed-yr-harn :	prob. from Treharne (pers. name)
Trosnant :	over the brook
trum :	a ridge or crest
Truman :	small ridge
Trum y Fawnog :	ridge of the place of peat
Trwyn Cilan :	trwyn (promontary); cilan (small ridge)
Trwyn y Bryn :	promontory of the hill
Tryfan :	high, pointed mountain
Tryfel :	triangular piece of land
Tryweryn :	a watering stream
Tudweiliog :	land of Tudwal (pers. name)
Twmpath :	a mound
Twmpathmelyn :	yellow mound
Twr-gwyn :	white tower
Twyn Llannan :	twyn—mound; llan—a church or village
tŷ :	a house
Tŷ-ar-y-graig :	house on the rock
Tŷ-bach :	little house
Tŷ-brith :	mottled house
Tycanol :	middle house
Tycerrig :	stone house
Tŷ-coch :	red house
Tŷ Cornel :	corner house
Tŷ-croes :	house on crossroads
Tŷ-crwyn :	house of skins
Tŷ Danydderwen :	house below the oak-tree
Tŷ-du :	black house
Tyddyn :	a small farm; cottage
Tŷ Faenor :	Chieftain's house; one made of stone
Tŷ-fry :	upper house
Tŷ-gwyn :	white house
Tyisaf :	lower house

Tyle-glas :	green hillside
Tylwch :	house of mud; home near pool
Tyllici (Tylleucu) :	house of Lucy
Tyn-y-groes :	farmstead of crossroads
Tŷ-llwyd :	grey house
Tŷ-mawr :	big house
Tŷ-nant :	house of stream or valley
Tynewydd :	new house
Tyn-y-bryn :	farm or cottage of the hill
Tŷ Pellaf :	farthest house
Tŷ-poeth :	warm house
Tŷ-rhos :	house of moorland
Tytandderwen :	house below the oak tree
Ty-top:	top house
Tyuchaf :	upper house
Tŷ y Banadl :	house of the broom (plant)
Tŷ-y-graig :	house of the rock
Tŷ-y-maes :	house of the meadow
tyn (tyddyn) :	a small farm or cottage

-coed (in wood)	-y-cefn (of hillside)
-cwm (in valley)	-y-cornel (of the corner)
-llwyn (of grove)	-y-ddôl (of meadow)
-pwll (of pool)	-y Fawnog (of peat land)
-rhos (of moorland)	-y-fron (of hillside)
-y-beili (of enclosure)	-y-ffordd (of road)
-y-berth (of hedge)	-y Gribin (of crest)
-y-bryn (of hill)	-y-groes (of crossroad)
-y-bryniau (of the hills)	-y Llidiard (of the gate)
-y-bwlch (of the pass)	-y-maes (of the meadow)
-y Byrwydd (of short wood)	-y Pistyll (of the well)
-y-cae (of the field)	-y-Pwll (of the pool)
-y-pwll (of the pool)	yrwtra (of the lane)
-yreithin (of the gorse)	-yr-ynn (of the ash trees)
-yrhedyn (of the fern)	y-twll (of the hole)
-y-rhyd (of the ford)	-y-waun (of the meadow)

Ucheldre :	high town or homestead
Uwchlaw'r-coed :	above the wood
Uwch-y-coed :	above the wood
Uwch y Garreg :	above the rock

Van (Fan) :	a peak
Vaynor (Faenor) :	chieftain's house; of stone
Velindre (Felindre) :	home of mill; township of villeins (serfs)
Venni-fach :	Prob. derived from Benni (pers. name)
Verwick (Ferwig):	barley grange
Vron (fron) :	hillside

Waun (gwaun) :	moorland or meadow
Waunclapiau :	moorland of hillocks
Waun Cwmcalch :	moorland of valley of lime

Waun-ddu :	black moorland
Waun-fach :	small meadow
Waun-fawr :	big meadow
Waun-gau :	meadow of hollow
Waun Lluest Owain :	moorland of Owain's lodging
Waunmarteg :	moorland of river Marteg (a horse)
Waun-oer :	cold moorland
Waun-wen :	white meadow or moorland
Waun-y-bwlch :	moorland of the pass
Waun-y-Gadair :	moorland of the camp
Waun-y-pant :	moorland or meadow of the hollow
Waun y Sarn :	moorland of the causeway
wen (gwen) :	white; fair; pleasant
Wenallt :	fair hillside or wood
Wern (Gwern) :	a marsh; alder trees
Wernewydd :	new alders or marsh
Wern Heulog :	sunny marsh
Wernog :	of alders or marshy
Wern y Blaidd :	marsh of the wolf
Wern-y-wig :	marsh of the wood or bay
Wig (gwig) :	a wood or bay
Winllan (Gwinllan) :	a vineyard
y :	the (before consonants)
Y Belan :	round hill
Y Berwyn :	name of mountain (white-topped)
Y Clogydd :	the knolls
Y Drain :	the thorns
Y Drenewydd	the new town
Y Drum :	the crest of a mountain
Y Ddraig Goch	the red dragon
Y Fan :	the peak
Y Felin :	the mill
Y Figyn :	the quagmire
Y Foel :	the bare hilltop
Y Freni :	land that juts out; fach - small; fawr - big
Y Ffridd :	the mountain pasture
Y Gadfa :	the place to drive animals
Y Gaer :	the fort
Y Garnedd :	the cairn
Y Glôg :	the crag
Y Glonc :	the protubering place
Y Golfa :	place of tree branches
Y Groes :	the cross or crossroads
Y Grug :	the heather
Y Gwernydd :	the marshes
Y Llethr :	the slope

Ynys :	river meadow or island
Ynys-hir :	long river meadow
Ynysmarchog :	meadow of horseman
Ynysyrwyddfa :	r. meadow of the grave
Yr :	the (before vowels)
Yr Allt :	the hillside or wood
Yr Allt Boeth :	the warm or burnt hillside
Yr Eifl :	gap of two peaks
Yr Oerfa :	the cold place
Yr Onnen :	the ash-tree
Yr Wyddfa :	(Snowdon); the grave (above ground)
Ysbyty Ifan :	hospice of Ifan
Ysgir-fawr :	river name (big ridge)
Ysgirfechan :	river name (little ridge)
Ysgubor :	barn
Ysguborion Cochion :	red barns
Ysgubornewydd :	new barn
Ysgubor Pen-y-bryn :	barn; hilltop
Ysgubor-y-coed :	barn of the wood
Ysgwd Ffordd :	waterfall of the road
Ystrad :	a vale; wide valley bottom
Ystradau:	flat area of land in river valley. Stradey and Strade, names given for the well-known rugby ground at Llanelli, are Ystradau wrongly spelt
Ystradfellte :	valley of river Mellte (swift)
Ystradgynlais :	valley of Cynlais (pers. name)
Ystradmarchell :	the vale of Marchell (pers. name)
Ystradmeurig :	valley of Meurig (pers. name)
Ystum Colwyn :	bend of river Colwyn (young animal)
Ystum Capel :	river bend of the chapel
Y Wenallt :	the fair slope or wood

and last but not least:—

Llanfairpwllgwyngyllgogerychwyrndrobwllllantysiliogogogoch

(St. Mary's Church of the pool of the white hazel near the rushing whirlpool, St. Tysylio's church, near the red cave).

More from Glamorgan and Gwent

aber :

mouth of a river usually followed by name of river

e.g. Afan (p. name)
Aman (per. name)
Bargod (border)
Big (peak)
Cannaid (white)
Carn (cairn)
Cregan (shells)
Dare : (Dâr-oaks)

Fan (peak)
Gavenny (smith)
Gwynfi (per. name)
Cynffig (per. name)
Pennar (high land)
Sychan (dries up)
Tyleri (per. name)

Allt-wen :	fair or white hillside
Allt-yr-ynn :	hillside of the ash-trees
Baglan :	saint's name
Bargoed (Bargod) :	a border
Barry :	prob. from "barr"—summit
Basaleg :	from "basilica" Latin for church
Bedlinog (Bodlwynog) :	home of the fox
Bedlinog:	probably BEDLWYNOG - place abundant with birch groves
Bedwas :	place of birch-trees
Bedwellte (Bodfelltau):	place of quick stream
Bedwelltey:	probably Bedw - birch trees; elltey - corruption of elltydd - hill sides
Beddau :	graves
Betws Newydd :	betws—prayer house; newydd—new
Blaenafon :	source of river
Blaen-cwm :	top end of valley
Blaendulais :	source of r. Dulais (dark water)
Blaen-garw :	source of r. Garw (rough)
Blaen-gwrach :	source of r. Gwrach (old hag)
Blaenllechau :	source of r. Llechau (rocks)
Blaenrhondda :	source of r. Rhondda
Bodringallt :	poss.: bod—home; rhingyll—sergeant
Bôn-y-maen :	foot of the rock
Brithweunydd :	mottled meadows
Briwnant :	valley or brook of ditch
Bryncethin :	hill of Cethin (pers. name)
Bryn-coch :	red hill
Brynmenyn :	hill; menyn—butter (rich land)
Brynna (Bryniau):	hills
Bwlch-y-clawdd :	pass of the mountain
Bwllfa :	place of pit or pool

Caerleon (Caer y Lleng):	Fort of the legion
Caer-went :	caer—fort; gwent—a field or plain
Canton :	town on r. Canna
Cardiff (Caerdydd):	fort on r. Tâf
Carn Celyn .	cairn of r. Celyn (holly)
Carreg Siglo :	rocking stone
Castellau :	castles
Castell Coch :	red castle
Castell Mynach :	castle of the monk
Cefn Mabli :	hillside of Mabli (pers. name)
Cefn Onn :	hillside of ash-tree
Cilfynydd :	mountain nook or r. source
Clydach :	r. name (rocky bed)
Clyn (Clun):	a meadow
Clwydyfagwyr :	gate of the rocks or walls
Coed-ar-hyd-y-glyn (Coedrhiglan):	wood of Rhiglan (pers. name)
Coed-cae :	wood field
Coed-duon :	black woods
Coedely :	wood of r. Elai (prob. pers. name)
Coed-pen-maen :	wood at head of rock
Coed-y-paun :	wood of the peacock
Cwrt yr Ala :	court of Raleigh
Craig-y-llyn :	rock of the lake
Craigyrefail :	rock of the smithy
Craig yr Eos :	rock of the nightingale
Creigiau :	rocks; cliffs
Crofft y Genau :	small field at opening
Croffty :	house of small meadow
Crymlyn :	valley with a bend
Crynant :	round-shaped valley
Cwm :	a bowl-shaped valley
Cwmaman :	valley of r. Aman
Cwm-brân :	valley of r. Brân (dark)
Cwmfelin :	valley of mill
Cwm-ffrwd :	valley of stream
Cwm-park :	valley of parkland
Cwmsymlog :	valley of wild strawberries
Cymer, y :	river confluence
Cyncoed :	chief or early wood
Deri :	oak trees
Dinas :	a fort or city
Dinas Powys :	dinas—fort; Powys—tribal land
Dowlais :	r. name—dark colour
Efailisaf :	lower smithy
Eglwysilan :	church of Ilan

Ely :	from Elái (river name)
Ewenny :	from name of a goddess (Aventi)
Felindre :	home of mill or home of villeins
Fochriw :	boch—cheek; rhiw—slope
Ffynnon-dwym :	warm spring
Ffynnon-y-gog :	cuckoo well or (coeg—empty)
Gabalfa :	from 'Ceubalfa'—a ferry
Gelli :	a small wood
Gellidawel :	quiet grove
Gelli-gaer :	wood of the fort
Gelli Fendigaid :	holy grove
Gilfach-goch :	red nook
Gilfach Rhyd :	nook of the ford
Glas-coed :	green trees
Glyncornel :	glyn—glen; cornel—corner
Glyncorrwg :	glen or r. Corrwg (short stream)
Glyn-neath (Glyn-nedd):	glen or r. Nedd
Glynogwr :	glen of r. Ogwr (swift)
Glyn-taff :	glen of. r. Taf (dark water)
Goetre-fawr :	home in wood; fawr—big
Gorseinon :	the marsh of Einon
Graig :	a rock or cliff
Groes-faen, y :	the stone cross
Gwent :	a field or plain
Gwernvale :	poss. gwern—marsh; moel—bare hill
	or from Goronwy Foel (pers. name)
Hendre :	main or winter dwelling
Hendreforgan :	home of Morgan
Hendresgythan :	home of wild pigeon
Hendy :	old house
Heol Gerrig :	rocky road
Heol-las :	green road
Hirwaun :	long meadow
Lisvane (Llys-faen):	stone court
Loughor (Llwchwr):	marshes; wet places
Llanbleddian :	church of St. Bleddian
Llancadle :	church of St. Cadell
Llancarfan (Nantcarfan):	border stream
Llandaff :	church on r. Taf
Llandefaelog:	church of St. Maelog
Llandough (Llandochau):	church of St. Dochau
Llanelen :	prob. church of Elen
Llanelli :	church of St. Elli
Llanfihangel Troddi:	St. Michael's church: Troddi—n.
	of river (strong)

58

Llanfoist (Llan-ffwyst):	church of St. Ffwyst
Llangennech:	church of St. Cennech
Llangennith (Llangynydd):	church of St. Cynydd
Llan-gwm :	llan—church; gwm—valley
Llangybi :	church of St. Cybi
Llanharan :	church of St. Haran
Llanhilleth:	church of St. Hilledd
Llanillterne :	church of St. Illteyrn
Llanishen :	church of St. Isien
Llanmadoc :	church of St. Madoc
Llanover :	church of St. Myfor
Llanrhidian :	church of St. Rhidian
Llan-soy :	church of St. Tysoe
Llantarnam (Nant	brook of Teyrnon
Teyrnon):	once the home of an abbey of that name. An older name was Nant Teyrnon - the stream of Teyrnon. Teyrnon was a fictitious prince of South Wales. See The Mabinogion, Book 1 by Owen Jones and Thomas Jones.
Llanthony (Llan Nant Hodni):	church of r. Hodni (pleasing)
Llantrisant :	church of three saints
Llantrithyd :	brook of Rhirid (pers. name)
Llantwit Faerdre :	church of Illtyd; faerdre — steward's house.
Llantwit Major (Llanilltyd Fawr):	big church of Illtyd.
Llanvetherine :	church of St. Gwytherin
Llanwarw :	church of St. Wynarwy
Llanwenarth :	church of St. Gwenarth
Llanwonno :	church of St. Gwynno
Llysworney :	court of Gwrinydd (pers. name)
Machen :	ma—plain; chen—from a pers. name
Maerdy :	house of steward
Maesaraul :	sunny meadow
Maes-bach :	little meadow
Maes-teg :	fair meadow
Maesycymer :	meadow of the river confluence
Magor (Magwyr):	stones; walls
Marcross :	march—horse; rhos—moorland
Melin Caiach :	mill of r. Caeach (border stream)
Merthyr Dyfan :	grave of St. Dyfan
Merthyr Tudful :	grave of Tudful the martyr
Morgannwg (Glamorgan):	land of Morgan
Mynyddislwyn :	mountain; Islwyn (pers. name)
Nant-garw :	valley of r. Garw (rough)
Nantgwyddon :	stream or valley of the witch
Nant-y-ffin :	stream of the border
Nant-y-glo :	stream or valley of the coal
Nant-y-moel :	stream or valley of bare hill
Neath (Nedd) :	river name (from Latin—nidum)

Nyth Brân :   nest of the crow

Pandy :   a fulling mill
Pant :   a hollow
Panteg :   fair hollow
Pant-y-graig-wen :   hollow of the white rock
Pembrey (Pen-bre):   hill top
pen :   head; end, chief; top

allt : slope		fer : short	
clawdd : ditch		rhys : pers. name	
Coed : wood		y-bont : of bridge	
craig : rock		ydarren : of rock	
dyrys : rough		y-fai : of field	
gam : crooked		y-garn : of mound	
llwyn : grove		ygarreg : of rock	
maen : rock		y-lan : of hill	
prysg : brushwood		y-waun : of meadow	
rhiw : hillside		yr heol : of road	
ceibr : rafter			

Pendoylan (deulwyn):   end of two groves
Penlle'r-gaer :   head of place of fort
Pen-mark (Pen-march):   pen—head; march—horse
Pen-rice (Pen-rhys):   head of Rhys
Pentre :   a village
Pentre-bach :   little village
Pentrepiod :   village of magpies
Plas-marl :   mansion : rich soil
Pontardawe :   bridge over river Tawe
Pontcanna :   bridge over r. Canna (white)
Pont-hir :   long bridge
Pontllan-ffraith: (-llyn-) bridge of mottled lake
Pontnewydd :   new bridge
Pontrhyd-y-fen :   bridge of ford of peak
Pontyates (Pont-iets):   bridge of gates
Pontybrenin :   bridge of the king
Pont-y-clun :   meadow of bridge (orig. Pont-y-clown)
Pont-y-gwaith :   bridge of the coal-mine
Pont-y-pool :   bridge of the pool
Pontypridd (-tŷ pridd):   bridge of earthen house
Pont-y-waun :   bridge of the meadow
Porth, Y :   the gateway
Porth-cawl :   poss. harbour of sea-cabbage
Porthkerry :   harbour of Ceri (pers. name)
Pwll-coch :   red pool
Pwll-gwaun :   pool of the meadow
Pwllmelin :   pool of mill

Pwll yr Hebog :	pool of the hawk
Pyle (Y Pil) :	tidal creek; pool
Pysgodlyn :	fish pool
Radyr :	prob. Aradur—a house of prayer
Raglan :	from Rhag (defensive) and glan (river bank)
Rassau (y Rasau) :	the mill leats (of old ironworks)
Resolven :	rhos—moor; soflen—corn stubble
Roath (Rhath) :	land near fort
Ruperra :	from rhiw—a hill; perrai—pears
Rhigos (Grugos) :	place of heather
Rhiw Saeson :	hill of the English
Rhondda :	from 'Rhoddneu'—a babbling stream
Rhoose :	prob. rhos—moorland
Rhosili (Rhos Sulien) :	moor of Sulien (pers. name)
Rhydfelen :	yellow ford
Rhydlafar :	rhyd—ford; lafar—babbling
Rhydfelin :	ford or brook of the mill
Rhyd-y-fro :	brook or ford of the vale
Rhyd-y-meirch :	ford of the horses
Rhymney :	river that burrows its way
Senghennydd :	land of Sangen (pers. name)
Sirhowy :	a river name (meaning not known)
Skenfrith (ynys Gynwraidd):	r. meadow of Cynwraidd
Skirrid (Ysgryd) :	rough
St. Lythan's (Llwyneliddon):	grove of Eliddon
Tafarnau-bach :	little taverns
Tai-bach :	little houses
Tairheol :	three roads or houses of road
Tal-y-garn :	headland of the cairn
Tal-y-waun :	headland of the meadow
Tan-y-bryn :	below the hill
Tarren y Bwllfa :	crag of place of pit or pool
Ton-du :	black lay-land
Tongwynlais :	lay-land of the white stream
Tonna :	lay-lands
Tonpentre :	ton—lay-land; pentre—village
Ton-teg :	fair lay-land
Tonypandy :	lay-land of the fulling-mill
Tonyrefail :	lay-land of the smithy
Trealaw :	home of song (or water lily)
Trebanog :	tre—homestead; bannog—of peaks
Tredegar (Tredegyr):	homestead of Tegyr
Trehafod :	summer home
Trefforest :	homestead in wild-open land

Tregynog :	home of Cynog
Treorci :	home of r. Orci or Orchwy
Trerhingyll :	home of the sergeant
Tresilian :	home of Silian (pers. name)
Troed-y-rhiw :	foot of the hill
Trostre :	over the town or homestead
Twyncarno :	hillock of cairns
Twyn-y-gwynt :	hillock of the wind
Tŷ-croes :	house on crossroad
Tŷ-draw :	house yonder
Tŷ-du :	black house
Tynewydd :	new house
Tyla Canol :	middle hillside
Tyla-fawr :	big hillside
Tyntyla :	small farm on the hillside
Tynyfforest :	small farm on open land
Tyn-y-graig :	small farm of the rock
Tyn-y-pant :	small farm of the hollow
Tyn-y-pwll :	cottage or farm of the pool
Waun Felin :	meadow of the mill
Wentloog (Gwynllwg):	a pers. name
Wern-ddu, Y:	the black marsh
Ynysangharad :	r. meadow of Angharad
Ynys-boeth :	ynys—river meadow; boeth—warm
Ynys-hir :	long island or r. meadow
Ynys-y-bwl :	ynys—meadow; bwl (pool or inn name)
Ystalyfera :	tal—end; fera—rick
Ystrad :	wide valley
Ystradyfodwg :	the vale of St. Tyfodwg
Ystradmynach :	the vale of the monk
Ystradowen :	the vale of Owen

How much do you know?

1. Give the English for:

Allt-mawr

Aber-nant

Aber-ffrwd

Aberystwyth

Berllan

Bryncelyn

Blaen-glyn

Brynawelon

2. Give the Welsh for:

fortress or camp

cold well

golden grove

lakeside

river mouth

red acre

little mill

the king's pound

3. Can you name six places containing the name of a tree.

4. How many places can you name which refer to a river or stream.

5. The word 'pen' has a number of meanings. How many do you know?

6. Give the English for:

caeau

Caban coch

Cae Mawr

Capel Celyn

Craig Pwll Du

Craig-y-nos

Crug-y-bar

Cwrtycadno

7. Give the Welsh for:

old house

green road

summer dwelling

rock or cliff

meadow of the mill

edge of the lake

a glade

church of St. Mary

8. Can you complete these names?
   tŷ-(small); tŷ-(big); tŷ-(black); tŷ (newydd)

9. How many names do you know that refer to water of some kind?

10. How many colours can you find in the place-names?

11. How many personal names do you remember?

12. What words denote different kinds of valleys?

13. Give the English for:

Dan-y-coed

Derwen

Dôl-fach

Drain

Dôl-las

Drum Ddu

Dolfelin

Dryslwyn

14. Give the Welsh for:

new mill   green valley
big ridge   crossroads
a ditch   river Severn
a recess   long stream

15. Name as many as you can of the saints mentioned in the place-names.

16. Can you give the complete Welsh names for:

> Pont (stile); Pont (of the cave);
> Esgair (middle); Rhyd (lime-kiln)

17. Which of these does not contain a saint's name:

Llanrhystud   Llan-faes   Llangeitho
Llangadog   Llansawel   Llan-y-cil
Llanddeusant   Llangurig   Llan-gors

18. Can you give some reasons why some Welsh words change in spelling?

19. Do you know the meaning of the place-names near your home?

20. Can you give the meaning of any place-names not mentioned in this book?